Rudolf Geser

**Classic Cycle Races
of Europe**

Classic Cycle Races of Europe

23 race routes to ride yourself

Rudolf Geser

 SBL Springfield Book Limited

British Library Cataloguing in Publication Data
Geser, Rudolf
    Classic cycle races of Europe: 23 race routes to
    ride yourself
    I Title II Adam, David
    796.6

ISBN: 1 85688 028 1

Cover design: Chris Hand, Design for Print
Translation: David Adam
Typesetting: Ocean Repro, Leeds
Maps: Kartographie Huber, Munich
Printed and bound by Colorcraft, Hong Kong

Photo credits

The author and publishers wish to thank the
following people:

R Kübler for the photograph on page 66
H Seidl for the photographs on
pages 14, 26, 44-45
P Witek for the photograph on page 15
Graham Watson for supplying the jacket
photography and photo on page 6

All other photography is by Rudolf Geser

Acknowledgements

The publishers are grateful to Steve Snowling
for his translation of Chapter 5 The Amstel
Gold Race.

Contents

Foreword

*T*here is no doubt that cycling as a pastime is more popular than ever. It's hardly surprising that it is also the most photogenic of pastimes too. Many of the routes suggested in this book have driven photogenic desires in me for more than a decade, whilst watching the classic one-day road races unfold in such timeless settings as on cobblestones, mud-churned lanes and back-breaking Ardennes hills, you become aware of a great tradition. Just as the conquerors of those races provide me with a wealth of heroic portraits, so it is that the courses themselves hold their own particular attractions, casting forth poignant images at each change in the light or weather, at each turn in the road ahead.

After the Spring tours there are always those trans-Alpine routes to savour as the national Tours of Italy and France make their way around their respective regions – forging heroes of another ilk, amidst a paradise of snow-capped mountains and breathtaking landscapes. Many of the Alpine *randonnée* routes are based on the very roads where riders carved their careers, and thus their names into the heart of cycling years ago. Today the most famous routes may take a particular champion's name as a mark of respect such as the Fausto Coppi–Cuneo (chapter 20).

This paradise of cycling terrain is open to any able and fit person who wishes to seek his own adventures along the classic cycling routes of Europe, from the near novice to experienced *randoneur*. And as you'll discover, by riding on any one of the routes offered in this book, the two distinct sides of road cycling – racing and touring – become as one. Whether you opt for a classic route such as the Tour of Flanders or the endurance test of Norway's Den Store Styrkeprøven, or indeed your own variation of any such route, the sensation is the same – pure exhilaration. While you may never achieve the stature of a Fausto Coppi, an Eddy Merckx, or a Louison Bobet, you will retrace their historical tracks and partake in a great adventure of your very own.

Graham Watson

The Giro d'Italia climbs away from Corvara amid the splendour of the Dolomites

Preface

What cyclist would not like to test his fitness probably gained after many hard training rides and hours in the saddle? or discover new routes and places with friends and fellow cyclists, or just gain fresh experience by taking on a new challenge? Cycle racing is one way of doing just that, but not everyone has the necessary qualities or *wants* to take on new challenges in the context of tough competition and have to pit themselves against other riders.

Cycle touring events are an alternative worth considering; they are organised events, but they allow a certain freedom for your own ideas and objectives. Without undue pressure to produce a performance – subject only to your own desire to do well – you are free to choose your own time and speed, with some routes you can even choose the distance you want to cover according to your ability. It does not matter when you reach the finishing line, as there you will find only winners, there are no losers.

Each year there are more than 1000 touring events held in Germany alone; they are mostly organised regionally by clubs who stage them with with great care and a suitable measure of idealism. This makes for a friendly atmosphere as several hundred cyclists, sometimes fewer, and mainly from the immediate area, gather together to set out on a clearly marked route – usually on the most attractive roads in the region – all for the cost of a very modest entry fee.

Some events, however, have succeeded in extending their fame beyond the boundaries of their region. Some profit from the fact that they follow in the tracks of a classic race as ridden by the professionals, others may impress you by their hill climbs, or the length of their route, and others purely by their scenic beauty. These routes form the highlights of many cyclists' season, long anticipated throughout the winter months, and for which the true cyclist will take out his bike for a training run, even in the bad weather of spring. You may well try some of them only once and decide that particular route is not for you, there are other races like the Säntis Tour, the Tour of Vorarlberg or the Tour of Lake Constance that can be entered into your diary year after year. Part of the pleasure is in discovering your own favourites.

In this book I have described 23 of the best-known events, and if you were to ask me to name the best I could not give you an answer. Each has its own attractions, and much depends on the conditions of that day, also on one's companions, or subjective impressions. I would never have thought that the Belgian tours, such as Omloop Het Volk and the Tour of Flanders, could make such an impression on me, but they did, partly because of the route and the landscape, but also because of the people. This is inspite of there being practically no feed stations, a lot of cobblestones and some short 'killer' climbs *en route*.

I have tried to give as realistic an impression as possible of each tour with my descriptions of the routes and the supplementary organisational information, along with the photography. Ideally you should ride them for yourself, and I wish you great success and enjoyment in doing so.

Rudolf Geser

Introduction

The following pages describe many well-known race routes, which, if you turn up at the right time on the right day you can ride as part of an organised event. All of the chapters give such information and it is intended to broaden your choice of when and where you go. On the other hand if you seek peace and solitude with your bicycle, but still want to see for yourself the Dolomites, or the cobbles of the Kwaremont, to name but two, the text, photos and maps will help you to prepare for your trip. Then again, if you simply seek a few moments escape from your armchair read on – the choice is yours.

If you do decide to participate in the events mentioned, please bear in mind that you take part at your own risk. The organisers are not liable for accidents or damage. It is therefore in your own interest to obtain third party insurance, possibly a sports medical examination, and above all to ride in a manner suited to your ability and fitness. Whilst every effort has been made to ensure the accuracy of the information here, changes at short notice to the organisation or running of the event or to conditions on the course cannot, of course, be ruled out. You should therefore request the latest information nearer the time of your planned trip in order to confirm the details of the event.

Staging a cycle touring event usually involves a lot of work, red tape and official permits issued conditionally and valid for only a limited time. Whether such a permit is issued again for the following year depends very much on the orderly running of the event. For this reason please follow the organisers' instructions and most importantly observe the Highway Code. Usually, routes are not closed off to general traffic and the Highway Code does apply. The unruly behaviour of a few participants ignoring the code can endanger future events.

Finally, a few requests: do not use support vehicles, prepare for the tour in accordance with its level of difficulty, and always wear a protective helmet. The following tips and suggestions are listed to help when preparing for your tour, and with careful planning your pleasure need not be spoiled by mistakes which could have been avoided.

Hints on preparation

Descents

Descents are dangerous. Gravel or sand on the bends, motorists or other cyclists represent danger which should not be underestimated. Crashes on fast descents can have extremely serious consequences. On long events the reduction in effort on the descent can often lead to lack of concentration. So always approach descents defensively and with great caution. Do not allow yourself to be tempted to keep up with faster riders, and always wear a crash helmet on descents.

Equipment

The best machine for these cycle touring events is a racing bike: the more refined its equipment the better. Routes of more than 200 kilometres with thousands of metres of hills to climb are a handicap, however good your equipment. It seems completely senseless to waste your strength unnecessarily on heavy, old equipment.

Recently, riders using mountain bikes have been seen on these difficult routes. Generally, mountain bikes have heavier wheels which, combined with increased tyre resistance, means the effort required is considerably more than with a comparable racing bike. Only extremely fit and well-trained riders are capable of surviving rides such as the Europa Cup Marathon on a mountain bike. The mountain bike is, and will remain, less than ideal, on demanding touring events.

Support Vehicles

These vehicles represent a danger to other competitors. In addition, your own sporting achievement is devalued if you have the opportunity to step into a support car at any moment. Unless you have special needs try to do without such vehicles.

It is mainly less fit competitors who cannot heed this advice. In any case, support vehicles should not travel the whole course a few metres behind riders just to be on hand immediately. If there is a mishap other riders will be prevented from overtaking easily, long queues of traffic will form, which can increase the danger to other cyclists. If you cannot manage without a support vehicle, then try to arrange to meet up at regular intervals at selected rendezvous points, such as checkpoints or feed stations. It would also be best if these locations could be approached by the support vehicle on roads which do not form part of the route.

Clothing

A good kit will probably consist of: cycling shoes, overshoes, socks, cycling shorts with chamois insert, long lycra leggings, short-sleeved jersey, long-sleeved jersey, light windproof jacket, heavier jacket, cycling gloves and mitts, waterproofs (jacket and trousers), headband, goggles and a protective helmet. How many of each depends on the duration of your trip, but make sure you have a complete change of fresh clothes at the end of the tour. You should now be ready to face any weather – at least in terms of clothing. Your outer clothing should be as bright as possible, not for the śake of 'posing' but to be more visible to other road users.

Spares

If you are a racing cyclist you will not want to be hampered by the weight of too many spares, but some spares are essential. If you are using one piece racing tyres you should try to carry two spares. For those using tyres with tubes, one additional inner tube, plus repair kit and tyre levers should suffice. Include the most useful Allen keys for your machine (normally 4mm 5mm and 6mm), and a screwdriver with reversible shaft for Philips and regular heads. You can tape some spare spokes to the seat stay. Should you damage spokes on the rear wheel you will need the necessary removal tool and the correct spanner to change the spoke, and for one piece hubs you need suitable gear-block dismantling tools. As a rule these are not exactly portable! There is though a small gear-block dismantling tool available (Libero by Velotech) which will fit in a saddlebag, but you need to familiarise yourself in advance with its emergency use. It is perhaps best, especially if you have any doubts, to restrict yourself to carrying a nipple key, which is then always to hand. If a spoke is damaged it is usually possible to compensate, at least on a temporary basis, for the pull of the missing spoke, so that you will still be able to finish your tour.

Training

Regular training is essential if you are to take part in a cycle touring event. It is not possible to make generalisations, since training depends to a great extent on your available time, the standard you set for yourself and your level of motivation. You should, however, train three or, preferably, four times a week, covering at least 250 kilometres a week, and therefore about 1000 kilometres each month. As April to September are suitable for regular cycling, in our latitudes at least, you should aim for an annual training schedule of 6000 to 7000 kilometres – this should prepare you for most events. For the tougher tours such as the Dolomite Marathon and the Ötztaler Marathon, the Super Brevet de Randonneur des Alpes, La Marmotte or the Trondheim–Oslo event, your usual training schedule, such as mentioned above, will not be sufficient, and should be significantly increased. Bear in mind that form and fitness only come after proper training and preparation. Unfortunately, when the first events take place in spring, you can still feel unprepared. So if you are planning a spring outing it is advisable to keep yourself fit through the winter months by substituting other sports such as jogging, cross-country skiing or multi-gym work. And try not to put on too much weight during the winter!

Weather

Your enjoyment of a cycle touring event will depend largely on the weather conditions. In

good accurate information for the near continent. If you consider the cost of travelling and overnight accommodation, only to abandon the tour because of continuous rain, then it makes sense to pay attention to the forecasts.

Slipstreaming

Slipstreaming is the norm during racing and touring events. To ensure fairness, however, everyone is expected to take their turn at the head of the group. Riding on the back wheels of a group who are not known to each other is not without danger, and demands constant attention. Unforeseen obstacles, irregularity of tempo or faulty changes of lead can result in dangerous situations or crashes. Safe slipstreaming can only be learned through practice and experience. This cannot be expected of all the tour participants. Don't hesitate to fall back into another group, especially if you think that the behaviour of one group is too reckless or too nervous. This also applies if you are hindering a faster group as a result of your own slower performance.

Accessories

If the start of a touring event takes place in darkness, then lights are essential. Battery powered front and rear lights, which can be fixed to the front forks, saddle tube or rear forks, are suitable. Just remember to take spare batteries.

If it is possible to fit a second bottle holder to your bike you should do so. Only by providing yourself with sufficient liquid can you avoid muscle cramps, fatigue, or lethargy.

A mileometer is a sensible accessory which is worth the investment. If you are aware of the distance already covered, and what distance remains, you will be able to pace yourself more effectively and relax and enjoy your ride.

With sensible, functional clothing you can withstand bad weather even on a long rainy tour. These two ladies climbing the Dovrefjell (Trondheim–Oslo) in the rain only have another 400 kilometres to go

bad weather or continuous rain the pleasure is seriously curtailed! Suitable clothing can be helpful, but hours of riding in the rain, and possibly in low temperatures, is not everyone's cup of tea. The weather cannot be influenced, but it can be forecast and the weather forecasting services of the German Meteorological Office provide information on regional weather conditions throughout Europe up to ten days in advance. This information, is very useful if your understanding of the German language is good. Alternatively you can telephone the British National Met Office (0344 85 4843) and they will give

Notes on the organisational information sections

For each tour the most important details are summarised under the title Organisational Information. They have been carefully researched, and to the best of our knowledge are correct. In the course of time, however, one detail or another will change, the author and publishers will try to incorporate any changes as soon as possible. Any suggestions for necessary changes resulting from your own experiences will be gratefully received, and will be included, if possible, in the next edition.

Date

Inclusion of an exact date is not possible, and dates of events can be changed within a restricted time range. Details of the month with a further indication of beginning, middle or end of that month do, however, give a good idea of the timing of the event. It is in the organisers' own interest to arrange the events on a similar date each year. Significant date changes are therefore not expected, although this is of course possible in exceptional cases. It is advisable to obtain application forms as soon as possible, and always check with the organisers well in advance.

Distance

The route length specified by the organisers is noted here. If there is a choice of route length, this is also indicated.

Total hill climbs

If the organiser gives details of total hill climbs, these are indicated. Otherwise, a calculation has been made by reference to map details. Problems only occur in respect of the Omloop Het Volk and the Tour of Flanders where topographical conditions make a calculation impossible. Towns whose altitudes are quoted on the maps are mostly situated on a hilltop. Between these points,

however, rolling countryside or short, steep climbs may be encountered. These can accumulate significantly over the total length of the route. The total hill climb figure has had to be estimated for both of these events.

Highest climb

Details of the highest climb should enable you to choose your gear ratios more easily.

Gearing

The details refer to the lowest gear used by myself. So 42 x 26, for example, means that during the tour I needed the 42 tooth front chainwheel, and as largest rear sprocket, one with 26 teeth. Since the correct gearing depends largely on the physical characteristics and state of fitness of the rider, two gearing suggestions are given where this seems necessary. In this case, use of the larger sprocket is strongly advised. These details are intended to be suggestions for you to consider.

Short but extremely steep climbs encountered mainly in the Belgian classics can present a problem. The steepest gradients are 18%, 20%, or even 22%. These sections are very short 50, 100, or at the most 200 metres long, and they only occur in two or three places at most on the entire route. Thus it is up to the individual rider to decide whether he can struggle up the climb using 42x26, push his machine if he has only 42x23

This trio has waited in vain for the rain to ease, caught on the high plateau of the Dovrefjell on the Trondheim–Oslo event they now must resign themselves to the hostile weather conditions

available, or whether he should fit a 28 tooth sprocket or larger, which will not be needed on the remaining 99% of the route.

Start place

In addition to details of the starting point, instructions on how to find it are included, if this seems necessary. If there is more than one starting point, these are detailed.

Accommodation

As a rule accommodation is available locally, but it is advisable to book rooms in advance. If a campsite is available this is indicated or if accommodation such as a sports hall with mattresses or a free campsite is offered by the organisers, this is indicated in the notes.

Start time

Start time details, such as staggered or early starts, are noted here.

Entry fee

You will see on the entry form whether reduced fees are available to young people or licence holders. There is usually an additional charge for late entrants. Entry fees vary greatly from event to event for example entry in the Tour of Flanders costs about £2, whereas the fee for the Europa Cup Marathon is around £20. This, of course, is connected with the cost of providing certificates, prizes, feed station or servicing facilities *en route*. During the Ötztaler Marathon, for example, six tons of food are provided for the feed stations. Along with the cost of servicing facilities, medical services and certificates for the participants, the entry fee will not cover all these expenses. Such an event is only possible with the financial help of sponsors. In contrast, the rider is left largely to his own devices on the Tour of Flanders, which does not, however, undermine the pleasure of riding it.

Feed stations

Feed stations are not always so well organised as for the Europa Cup Marathons. In many events, as in all the classics, there is no food, or virtually no food, available. A can of lemonade and a waffle, as on the Tour of Flanders, are, considering the minimal entry fee, a nice gesture from the organisers, but it is in no way sufficient for riders trying to survive the rigours of the course. In such cases you must carry your own provisions or obtain food in the cafés or restaurants along the route. Please remember that by applying early you will make it easier for the organiser to plan the necessary catering.

Participants

The numbers quoted by the organisers are noted here and are a good guide to the size of the event.

Contact address

You can obtain up to date information and application forms from the address provided.

Further information

Any special points of interest about the organisation or running of the event are noted here.

The Classics

*I*n the cycling world the classics are those cycle races which, because of their tradition and fame amongst the ranks of cycling enthusiasts, enjoy a high profile. Races such as Paris–Roubaix, Milan–San Remo or the Tour of Flanders are household names to any enthusiastic road-racing cyclist; and for a professional, a victory in such a race will surely count as one of the highlights of his career, only to be exceeded by victory in one of the really big tours, such as the Tour de France or the Tour of Italy.

Most classics take place in the spring, when a rider's competitive form is still not established, and the work of the professionals is made more difficult by poor weather conditions in addition to a really testing route. Belgium, a country with a deeply rooted cycling tradition, is the host to the majority of these classics. Racing enthusiasts have the opportunity to experience these race routes in the form of cycling events, and nowhere else can you get a better impression of the sheer sporting achievement of the professionals. Even the atmosphere is special; events are organised on the original routes where cycling history is made annually, and the chance to participate is a real thrill. Anyone who can overcome the difficulties presented by tough terrain and bad weather, can be just as proud of his achievement as the winner of the professional equivalent. On the following pages seven of the best known classics are described, of which four take place in Belgium, and one each in France, ltaly and the Netherlands.

An impression of the professional's Omloop Het Volk. Fortunately, there are only about five kilometres of these cobblestones to survive in total

Belgium: the stronghold of cycle racing. Every year countless spectators are attracted here to follow the action from the roadside

Omloop Het Volk ▬▬▬ 1

Belgium

*A*t six o'clock in the morning in the cafeteria of the Rozebroeken Sports Centre in St Amandsberg, a suburb of Ghent, there's just a handful of early risers filling in their registration forms and paying a modest entry fee to take part in the other Omloop Het Volk. Gradually the car park fills up, and as the new arrivals make preparations to start, the first cyclists are already following the small white arrows which will lead them through the sleeping streets of Ghent. It is already light in the capital of east Flanders, and the street lighting is off, but alongside the docks and canals, where the loading cranes loom motionless, the dockside rails demand considerable caution. The cyclists soon leave the town behind (8.5km) to emerge into the flat landscape along main roads, which run dead straight past sugar beet, and vegetable fields, and small single-storey brick cottages. The cycle paths in this area, separated from the main road by a white line, are not very wide, and it's as well to be aware that the poor road surface demands concentration, especially when cycling at speed.

In Deinze (25km) the first cobblestones appear. Admittedly there are only two sections of 100 metres each, but anyone who would like to find out more about my experiences of them should read the descriptions of the Tour of Flanders or Paris–Roubaix. In Desselgem (42.5km) the route follows sideroads whose condition is not much better than that of the cycle paths, and after Vichte (47.5km) we turn left by way of a small underpass, to encounter the first slight gradient. There's no need to change gear on the front mech, just shift to a bigger sprocket to deal with the 4% gradients, which are followed by similar descents and long level sections.

The expansive wooded hilltop of the Mont de L'Enclus marks the beginning of the East Flanders Uplands which cover the area south of Ghent between Schelde and Dender. Why these hills, which rise hardly 150 metres above sea level, are feared amongst racing cyclists – almost more than the highest Alpine passes – becomes apparent when a narrow road with a tarmacadam surface is reached at the foot of the Mont de L'Enclus (76.5km). The gradient, at first 8%, increases to about 12% after 500 metres, but much more unpleasant is the fact that the smooth road surface changes to cobblestones, and the effort needed to overcome the gradient must now be redoubled in order to keep the bucking front wheel more or less in contact with the road and heading in the right direction. So catastrophic are the cobbles that even a narrow, hollowed concrete gutter on the left-hand side of the road, which under normal circumstances would be ignored, offers a welcome means of escape.

After 300 metres, a short eternity so to speak, the sign for Kwaremont appears. The next 300 metres takes us past farms and small-holdings and to our next descent, but the cobblestones continue for another 100 metres as far as the junction with the main road. Shortly after crossing this road the Café de Oude Hoeve (79km) is reached, and with it the first checkpoint.

After this cobblestone section the ride to Geraardsbergen is pure relaxation. The gradient hardly increases to more than 6%, and on the long descents higher speeds could be reached if it were not for the constant changes of direction. A real test, however, awaits the rider at the Muur de Grammont, the infamous 'Wall of Geraardsbergen'. A row of houses on the eastern bank of the Dender (114km) leaves room for a narrow street. Our first signal to what lies ahead is the word 'MUUR' written in clear letters on the asphalt surface. After 400 metres on the 12% gradient the route turns off into a side street which shortly becomes a narrow cobbled lane. The gradient continues to increase and reaches 18%, when the road leads into a dark, shady avenue of trees for 200 metres. Not all of the cyclists cope with this section and they have to push their bikes to the tiny lake at the top of the hill (115km).

The next checkpoint on the Bosberg (121km) is reached without difficulty, except for the 400 metre long, 10% cobblestone climb at the end of the section.

After the Muur, further effort is required for the one kilometre 10% climb in Brakel (142km). With its meadows surrounded by barbed wire fences, where black and white cows graze, the crop fields are separated by low protective hedges, lines of high poplars and scattered copses; the landscape here in the Flemish Ardennes hardly offers great variety, but it is never monotonous, and the

The Muur von Grammont – the Geraardsbergen Wall – seems rather tame on the lower section at 12% and belies the 18% gradient and cobblestones that lurk ahead

heavily built-up areas do not produce a feeling of claustrophobia. The route remains much the same: slight gradients not usually more than 6%, with long descents and level sections which allow speedy progress, while the excitement is provided by cobblestones and short 'killer climbs'. Two of these are encountered at Leberg (150km) and the Berendries (154km), but without the cobblestones the short 14% climbs are not so bad.

The last checkpoint at the Café Oud Belgie (175km) is set back a little from the road and can be easily missed, as can the narrow, half-hidden lane which leads up to the Molenberg from here. After 300 metres of cobbles with a gradient increasing to 14% at the steepest point, the last steep section is completed next to a small farmstead (176km). Most riders will be able to contain their grief on realising this fact, for so early in the year any lack of training makes itself quickly felt, and it is good to know that there is only one more 400 metre cobbled section. By Merelbeke (200km) the slight gradients become ever fewer, and eventually the route flattens out completely. Greater concentration on the line of the route is needed at this stage, but those who have not lost sight of the arrows up to this point will surely find their way back to the starting line through the final maze of streets (212km).

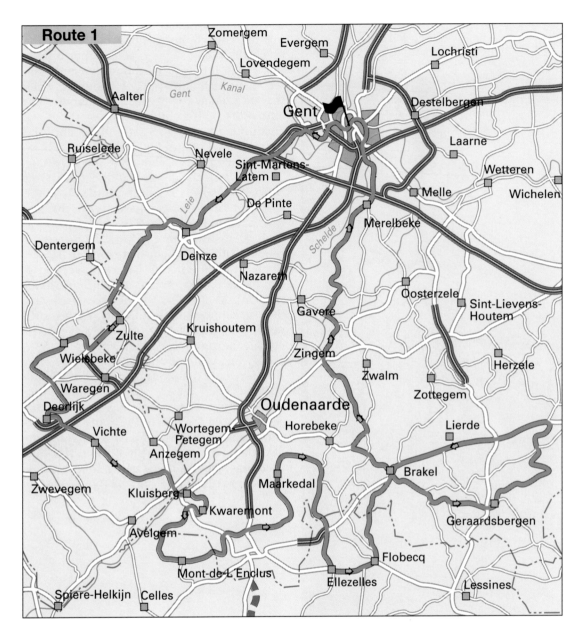

Route 1

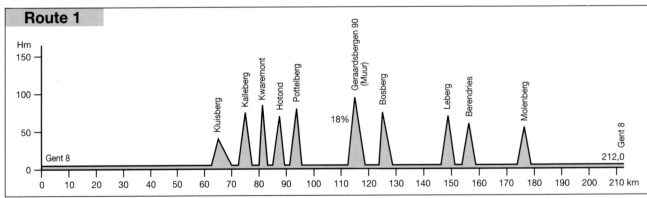

Route 1

Hm

150

100

50

0

Gent 8

Kluisberg

Kalleberg

Kwaremont

Hotond

Pottelberg

Geraardsbergen 90 (Muur)

18%

Bosberg

Leberg

Berendries

Molenberg

Gent 8

212,0

0   10   20   30   40   50   60   70   80   90   100   110   120   130   140   150   160   170   180   190   200   210 km

Organisational Information

Date – Mid May

Distance – 212km and 60km

Total hill climbs – Approximately 1300 and 200 metres

Highest climb – Approximately 200 metres at 18% on the Muur Geraardsbergen. Six other short climbs between 10% and 14%

Gearing – 42x26/28

Start place – Rozebroken Sports Centre in St Amandsberg, Ghent. Entering from the direction of Brussels take the Melle/Merelbeke (Ring 4) exit and then leave the motorway at exit 3 (Lokkeren/Oostakker). Turn left at next traffic lights towards Ghent. After about 3km a narrow road to the sports centre branches off to the left between the Aral and Poema service station

Accommodation – Hotels in Ghent. If in doubt, follow the tourist information office signs (green sign with white letter i) where you can obtain a hotel directory

Start time – Appointed start times between 6am and 8am

Entry fee – 100 Belgian francs

Feed stations – A drink, a piece of cake and a pot of yoghurt are distributed at one of the checkpoints

Participants – About 600

Contact address – WTC Gentse-Velospurters, Eeckhout Driesstraat, 89 B-9040 Gent Oostakker, Belgium

Further information – The route is indicated by white arrows and a letter V on the road surface. The tortuous nature of the route makes it advisable to stay in contact with riders who have some local knowledge. Cobblestones cover about 5km of the course

Narrow, poorly maintained, but usually traffic free roads make up a large part of the route in east Flanders

Liège–
Bastogne–
Liège
Belgium

2

At Whitsuntide, the small roadside village of Tilff, just south of Liège in the Ourthe valley is taken over by cyclists. Every year almost 7000 riders take part in the greatest and most difficult Belgian classic, the Liège–Bastogne–Liège (this amateur version of the race is known locally as the Tilff–Bastogne–Tilff). It is not easy to explain just why, of all the cycling events which follow in the tracks of the professional classics, this one in particular should enjoy such popularity. It could not be because of the faultless organisation: the cyclist is left largely to his own devices, as in all such Belgian events. And the scenery alone could not be the reason, the Ardennes, a heavily wooded range of hills – rising to almost 700 metres – with deep river valleys are indeed charming, but then so is the rest of Belgium's landscape, such as the hills and plains of Flanders around Ghent. The explanation lies in the 3515 metres of hill climb which represent a considerable total for the Belgian and Dutch riders, who are mostly unaccustomed to the mountains. Indeed, participation in this tour bestows certain prestige upon anyone who has overcome its challenges.

At four in the morning the first riders stand around in the darkness of the closed off main street, waiting for a larger group to gather. It's only when the organisers open up the street, and after some frenzied activity where everyone has his start card stamped, that the village houses disappear into the distance. The majority of us do not start until after five when there is sufficient daylight. Not that there is much to see in the immediate area, the flat road is the most remarkable aspect of the first three kilometres alongside the river, and this is to be the last level stretch of road that we can hope to enjoy for quite a while.

We follow the road, which branches off after Méry, for some time and get our first taste of what awaits us. For the first three kilometres the road climbs at 5% through the brush-covered slopes on the left-hand side of the valley as far as Dolembreux (7km). At the summit there are red brick houses and farmsteads, meadows, pastures with black and white cows and scattered copses. For a short time the road levels out somewhat, as it leads to Sprimont (7km) it continues to rise gently

Descents followed by gentle climbs on the road to Bastogne, keep bunches of riders intact

before descending at 8% into the village. Following an 8% climb out of the village for one kilometre there is a lengthy descent to Aywaille (11km). After a bridge over the Amblève river and two sharp bends through the village, the road climbs gently but unmistakably as far as Harzé (15km).

To confirm that we have journeyed south there is a distinct change in the architecture as can be seen in the grey stone blocks of the castle walls. The surroundings become more rural and the view across the Ardennes opens up. The route continues through open, picturesque meadows, briefly through leafy woodland sections, and down into little valleys with their grey shale-strewn hillsides. Climbs and descents alternate constantly, but the gradients hardly ever exceed 5%.

Beyond Deux-Rieux (30.5km) the River Aisne is crossed no fewer than four times in rapid succession. After Dochamps (45km) the road again rises gradually to a crossroads, which is soon followed by the first checkpoint located in a section of forest beyond Samrée (57.5km). There follows several gentle climbs and descents through open, rolling countryside between meadows, pastures and copses on the approach to Nadrin. Then down to Mormont (67.5km), a narrow bridge over the Ourthe and a two kilometre climb of 7% out of the valley, levelling off to rolling countryside as far as Longchamps (77.5km). The signpost for Bastogne comes into view, but after a descent of another kilometre, an 8% climb still separates us from our second checkpoint stamp, obtained from the Porte de Treves Sports Centre (85km).

Soon the main road can be left for the largely traffic free side-roads which criss-cross the sparsely populated hills of this area close to the Luxembourg border. Climbs and descents varying in length between 100 metres and one kilometre follow in regular rhythm, but mostly the gradient averages a comfortable 5%. Occasionally the climbs and descents increase in severity, as they do in the dense forests just before Brisy (110km), where once the Eburi and the Treviri sought sanctuary from Caesar's Legions in the Gallic Wars. The climbs are neither long nor severe enough to split up the groups which have clung together in tens and twenties, and so they arrive in

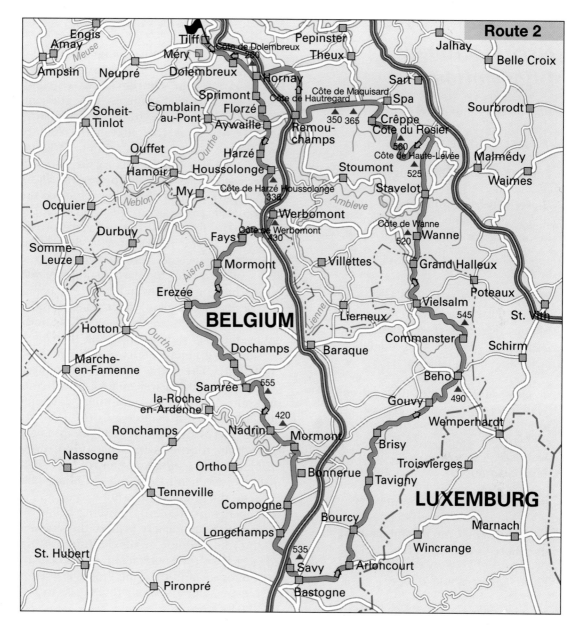

Engis
Amay
Ampsin
Neupré
Soheit-Tinlot
Ouffet
Hamoir
Ocquier
Durbuy
Somme-Leuze
Hotton
Marche-en-Famenne
la-Roche-en-Ardenne
Ronchamps
Nassogne
St. Hubert
Pironpré

Tilff
Méry
Dolembreux
Côte de Dolembreux 260
Comblain-au-Pont
Sprimont
Florzé
Aywaille
Harzé
Houssolonge
My
Fays
Mormont
Erezée
Dochamps
Samrée 655
Nadrin
420
Mormont
Compogne
Longchamps
535
Savy
Bastogne
Ortho
Bonnerue
Tenneville

Hornay
Côte de Hautregard
Côte de Maquisard
Remou-champs
Côte de Harzé Houssolonge 336
Werbomont
Côte de Werbomont 430
Villettes
Baraque
Lierneux

Pepinster
Theux
Sart
Spa
Crêppe
350 365
Côte du Rosier
560
Côte de Haute-Levée
525
Stoumont
Stavelot
Côte de Wanne
520
Wanne
Grand Halleux
Vielsalm
545
Commanster
Beho
490
Gouvy
Brisy
Tavigny
Bourcy
Arloncourt

Jalhay
Belle Croix
Sourbrodt
Malmédy
Waimes
Poteaux
St. Vith
Schirm
Wemperhardt
Troisvierges
Marnach
Wincrange

BELGIUM

LUXEMBURG

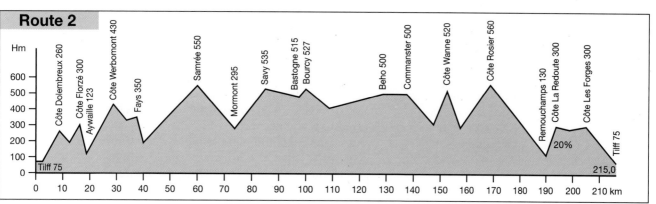

Hm

Tilff 75
Côte Dolembreux 260
Côte Florzé 300
Aywaille 123
Côte Werbomont 430
Fays 350
Samrée 550
Mormont 295
Savy 535
Bastogne 515
Bourcy 527
Beho 500
Commanster 500
Côte Wanne 520
Côte Rosier 560
Remouchamps 130
Côte La Redoute 300
Côte Les Forges 300
Tilff 75
20%
215,0

Organisational Information

Date – Whit Sunday

Distance – 215 kilometres

Total hill climbs – 3515 metres

Highest climb – Approximately 300 metres at 20% when climbing La Redoute in Remouchamps

Gearing – 42x26/28

Start place – Tilff, south of Liège. Take the Liège/Maastricht exit if approaching on motorway from Aachen. Then follow E25 in direction of Liège signposted 'Ardennes' as far as exit 41 (Tilff/Amoir)

Accommodation – Hotels in and around Tilff. There is a low cost campsite in the local park (no showers or hot water)

Start time – Appointed start times between 4am and 7am

Entry fee – 150 Belgian francs

Feed stations – Cans of lemonade are distributed from one of the checkpoints

Participants – About 7000

Contact address – Velo Club Tilffois, Route de Mery 25, 8-4050, Esneux, Belgium

Further information –The route is marked 'TBT' on the road surface. When registering for the event, a map showing the route for support vehicles, including rendezvous points is available for 5 francs. An accompanying diagram shows profiles of the last seven climbs on the course

Vielsalm in the Salm valley (141km) mostly intact.

The situation soon changes in Grand Halleux (147km), where we leave the valley; the road past the church seems to climb almost to the heavens with its 13% gradient. After 200 metres the course eases a little before starting the 13%, 400 metre climb to the Côte de Wanne. Easing again to 10% and then to 5%, the road leads to the summit. Here, just before the checkpoint (151.5km), any support vehicles which have ignored the ban on their presence are diverted from the road by the marshals. This measure proves necessary as the road down to Stavelot is steep and dangerous, with descents of up to 15% – many a rider has parted company with his machine on the hairpin bends.

In Stavelot (156km) there is more traffic, cobblestones and a one kilometre 12% gradient leading out of the village. This then levels off somewhat before we leave the main road (159.5km). The long descent to La Reid (164km) provides a welcome respite, before the route again climbs punishingly for some 560 metres at an even 7% to the Côte du Rosier (168.5km). This is the highest point of the whole tour. Passing through Crêppe (175km) the route descends for some distance. Even on the Côte du Maquisard (180km) the gradient does not exceed 7%. In Remouchamps (190km), huddling below the pillars of the motorway bridge, the dreaded climb of La Redoute awaits the riders. At the edge of town the route again passes beneath the motorway and then the gradient leaps to 12%, eases somewhat, only to increase to 20% for 300 metres.

Spectators gather here, forming a seething guard of honour, and hardly leaving room for the exhausted riders, who struggle up the climb before it eases to 14%. Finally, after 400 metres, the nightmare is at an end. Quite a few of us recover at the foot of a small stone monument just below the summit, which is marked by a tall, slender concrete tower. The road to Sprimont is easier, but there is another one kilometre 8% climb out of the village, a long descent to Forges, where the route branches off to the left, and then the last climb past the church to the

crossroads. At this stage many riders would swear that the climb is longer and steeper than one kilometre at 10%. We can enjoy the long descent to Méry, for there are no more climbs to come. Finishing in the Ourthe valley, we recognise this descent as the first climb at the start of the tour. Soon the outskirts of Liège appear and lead us back to the start (215km). The first riders are expected at 1.30 pm, but the stragglers do not finish until early evening.

25

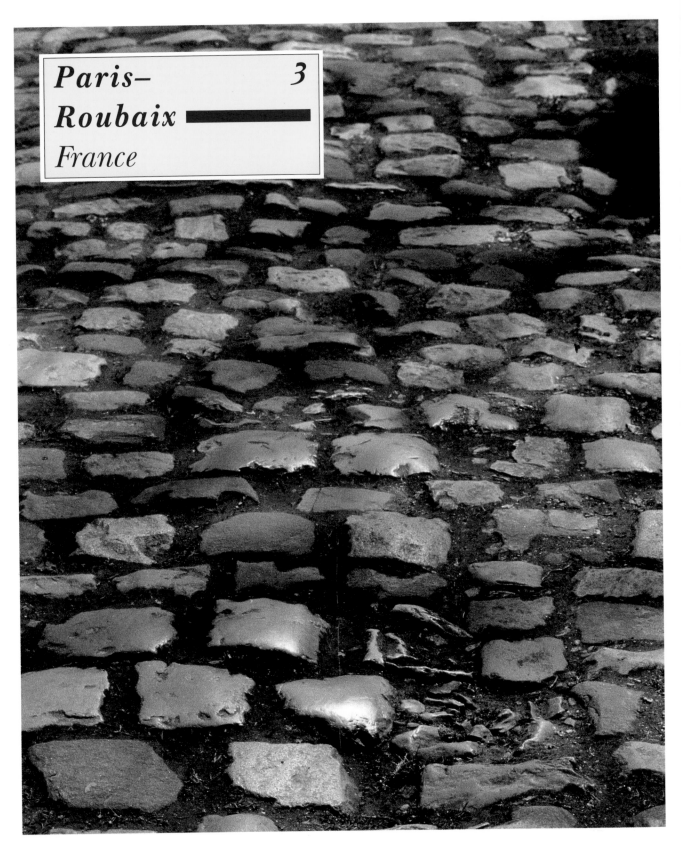

Paris–
Roubaix ━━━━━ 3

France

There was no cycle tour which had worried me – if not frightened me – so much as the Paris–Roubaix. Everything I had heard or read about it was in no way encouraging. People talked about the 'Hell of the North', about the most difficult of all the classic tours, about wind, rain, breakdowns and accidents. The length of the tour was not a problem: 265 kilometres is a considerable distance, but not an impossible one. Climbs were never cited as posing a difficulty. The contours of the route are more or less flat. So only the *pavés* remained, those stretches of cobblestone which the professionals fear more than the most difficult climbs in the Alps or the Pyrenees, and about which touring cyclists can tell some real horror stories. In the meantime I had discovered these cobblestones for myself on the Tour of Flanders in Belgium. There were hardly 10 kilometres of *pavé* there, but here we were faced with 57 kilometres. And if you remember that each metre on the cobblestones is one metre too many, then you have some idea of what awaits you.

At three o'clock in the morning, I find myself standing in a throng of several hundred other riders in the car park of the Centre de Rencontre de la Victoire in Compiègne (0.0km), waiting to be pushed forward to the two wooden tables which leave a narrow gap between the barriers, I have just fitted some battery lights to my bike, and in addition to the spare tyre in the saddlebag I have stowed away two inner tubes in the back pockets of my jersey. A rubber stamp on my start card, and then off we go into the pitch black night. The lights are essential, but they are barely strong enough to pick out the yellow arrows and the letters 'PR' on the road surface, and so you rely on the riders ahead. Some riders are luckier, and their way is illuminated by support cars, which according to the regulations are not allowed, but in fact are diverted from the route only twice by the marshals. At the start the route is flat, then the road climbs a little now and again, but the gradient is enough to make itself felt. Street lamps provide some light in only a few of the larger villages, and then we are once again swallowed up by the darkness, which continues until we reach the first checkpoint at the brightly lit football stadium in St Quentin (63km).

We have been riding for a good two hours when daylight first appears around 6.30am. A narrow, grey streak on the horizon slowly pushes away the darkness as we start out again. It's only now that we become aware of our surroundings: the country landscape of Picardy, used almost entirely as arable land to produce wheat, barley, rye and sugar beet.

The roads run dead straight through

The picture says it all! The feared cobbles that characterise Paris–Roubaix

This is not the only puncture which these two Italian riders from Milan have suffered today

27

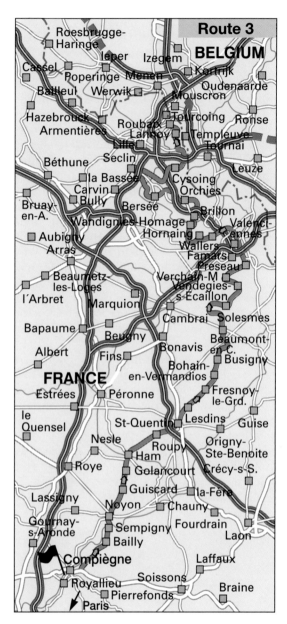

Troisvilles (99km). This is the first of 30 sections, of which the longest is 3.9 kilometres and the shortest 200 metres, and which amount to exactly 57.3 kilometres before the finish. Anyone who has ever worked with a heavy pneumatic drill can more or less imagine how you are shaken about on these sections, but you could understand the situation better if you put yourself in the place of the drill. There is no thought of riding faster, for the bumping, even at walking speed, is unbearable. First I try the middle of the slightly convex road surface, and then move over to one side, only to decide in the end that only the few centimetres of earth at the edge of the cobbles are tolerable, but this would be transformed into an impossible quagmire in rainy weather. These sections are not always flat, sometimes there is a slight gradient, which poses no problem, you can easily deal with this on a large sprocket. It is worse when the slope is downhill, then the greatest concentration and care is required: after the first few metres my water bottle flies from the bike, and then the battery lamp fixed to the front forks clatters on to the cobbles, whilst the rear lamp somehow gets caught between the rear forks and the brake mounting. I try and stow everything in my jersey pockets, where there is no room because of the two inner tubes.

Between the second checkpoint in Solesmes (118.5km) and the third in Valenciennes (149.5km) the *pavés* do not seem to succeed each other so closely as before, so that there is more time to recover between them. Nevertheless my speedometer is vibrated from its mounting, its casing cracked, and then I have my first (and only) puncture. After Valenciennes there is a noticeable change in the scenery. Indeed, the meadows, mostly used as grazing pastures for cattle, are used here as arable land, but everything here is more confined – more built up – the countryside is no longer so open as before. The gradients have almost disappeared. The new surroundings are as flat as a board, and with the best will in the world could not be described as the 'Hell of the North', cycling along such peaceful lanes could even be fun if it were not for the *pavé*, which seems unending and it feels like not one has been left out. These sections have

open countryside past green fields and brown ploughed acres which are interspersed with the yellow splashes of rape fields and a few scattered trees. At 3%, 4% or even a short 5%, the road rises for a few hundred metres to a hilltop from which we can see the next one up ahead, and then we descend a similar gradient, but at double the speed.

Nothing special to report so far: the roads have been good, the occasional easy gradients creating no problems until we come across the first cobbles beyond

Organisational Information

Date – Mid May

Distance – 265 kilometres

Total hill climbs – Hardly any climbing is involved

Highest climb – 5% on some short stretches during the first third of the course

Gearing – 52x21 or 42x19

Start place – Compiègne, about 75km north of Paris. From the motorway, the Centre de Rencontre de la Victoire is reached following the red signs with black arrows. Otherwise, follow the signs to the 'Hospital St Joseph' from the town centre, then look out for signs to 'Centre de Rencontre de la Victoire'

Accommodation – Hotels and campsites in Compiègne

Start time – Appointed start times between 3am and 5am

Entry fee – 50 French francs

Feed stations – At the time of writing only drinks were supplied at the checkpoints, except for the checkpoint in Orchies where some fruit and a muesli bar were available

Participants – About 1500

Contact address – Velo Club de Roubaix, 73 Avenue du Parc des Sports, F-591000 Roubaix or M Philippe Guilluy, 1 Rue Monplaisir: F-59390 Lannoy, France

Further information – The organisers offer transport for riders and their bikes from Roubaix to Compiègne on the day before the event, and from Roubaix to Compiègne afterwards. Departure times, prices and booking forms can be found within the information pack. It is possible to send luggage from Compiègne to Roubaix. The 'Tourist Formula' provides the option of starting in Compiègne on Saturday, spending the night in Solesmes after 118 kilometres, and continuing the tour to Roubaix on Sunday, starting between 8am and 9am. Tyres are available at the checkpoint's two service stations which can also carry out minor repairs. At the time of writing there were 57 kilometres of *pavé* to survive

nothing at all to do with cycling, and normally it would never occur to anyone to ride a single metre of them. It is simply the challenge of Paris–Roubaix that makes any sense of our efforts. After Wallers (164km) there is a section closed off to traffic so all support cars are diverted. Another stretch of *pavé* which passes through a grove of beech trees for about two kilometres. During the professional race thousands of spectators stand here, but today we share a narrow strip of earth next to the cobbles with a few joggers and walkers.

The last checkpoint is at Orchies railway station (191km), but it's no reason to breathe a sigh of relief – if we are to believe the information on our race card there are still another 16 *pavé*s to come, amounting to 26 kilometres. There is no reason to doubt what we've been told, especially after completing a particularly long, severe section on the outskirts of the village. The length of the sections makes itself felt: there are saddle sores and neck problems, but worst of all your fingers are tested. The handlebars must be held in a vice-like grip, and eventually your fingers begin to burn and go into cramp.

There is good reason for riders to wear thickly padded winter gloves, despite the fine weather, simply to minimise the worst jarring on the hands. We all begin to suffer at some point, but we suffer willingly, and we do not

suffer alone. That makes it all bearable. Even in Lannoy (267km) just before the finish, we are diverted on to side-roads around the town so as not to miss the last two 200 metre cobbled sections. Then the inconspicuous Roubaix boundary sign appears, along with the road to the velodrome in the park. A marshal points out the entrance (265km) and a long bend leading directly to the entrance of the race track, where barriers hold back the spectators, mostly friends and relatives. On the last lap of the track there are faces showing signs of the long day's ride, but they are full of contentment and rightly proud of their achievement. Despite the hard effort we are the richer for this experience, and many, who during the day have sworn never again to ride another metre over cobblestones, will at some time come back and ride it all again.

This year there was a total of 57 kilometres of cobblestones to negotiate

Flèche Wallonne 4
Belgium

The climb of
La Redoute at
Remouchamps is
tackled early in the
morning, maybe it's
as well for the
gradient over the
last 100 metres is a
good 14%

*A*longside the Liège–Bastogne–Liège race, Flèche Wallonne ranks as the second greatest cycling classic of the Belgian Ardennes. The Celtic word 'ardu' means high, precipitous, steep, but with heights hardly reaching 700 metres, these descriptions of the range of hills on the border between France, Luxembourg and Germany do not really ring true. Only the adjective steep is accurate, since the sharpest gradients do indeed reach 20%. But it is neither the steepest gradients nor the total hill climb figure that make this tour so difficult, but rather the constant climbs and descents which drain the strength from the riders' legs, far more so than the longest climbs on the highest Alpine passes. There is little to choose between Liège–Bastogne–Liège and Flèche Wallonne, for they hardly differ in length or total hill climb. The main difference between them is the fact that Flèche crosses the Ardennes from west to east, whereas Liège–Bastogne–Liège travels from north to south. At some points the two routes even coincide.

At five o'clock in the morning, still in darkness, the first riders are fixing start numbers to their frames. On leaving the park (0.0km) their race card is stamped and they ride along the dead straight road through Spa. Soon the main road is left behind and at the next junction (5km) the first climb begins. This finishes after 2.5 kilometre with a very regular 6% gradient on the Côte de Maquisard (7.5km), and provides a first impression of the typical landscape in this region: meadows with barbed wire fences, bushy hedges and lines of trees cross the countryside haphazardly, alternating with dark patches of forest. The two kilometre descent is followed by a climb of similar length, again at 6%, to the Côte de Hauregard (11.5km), leading immediately to a long descent into Remouchamps (16km). And then it's down to the nitty-gritty: the climb of la Redoute lies ahead. Gradually it has become lighter, and the small yellow arrows on the road surface can be made out more clearly, they lead us alongside the Amblève for a while and then under the motorway and out of town. This climb is 1.6km in length, starting out at 10%, increasing to 20% for 300 metres after one kilome-

tre, and easing back to 11% before rising another 100 metres at 14% leading to a fork a short distance below the summit. Most riders catch their breath here and watch the others fighting their way up the climb, before they tackle the steep descent ahead.

The route continues through sleepy villages, open meadows and stretches of forest, with climbs and descents, mostly of around 6%, but sometimes a little steeper, as in Hony (36km), where the road leads out of the village, climbing for one kilometre at 12%.

Hardly a car disturbs us in these early morning hours on the side-roads; we encounter more traffic on the main roads, which are followed briefly or, for the most part, just crossed. After Hody (55km) the countryside seems to open up: agri-cultural areas have pushed back the forests, and even the lengthy climbs and descents change to a gentle undulation. We catch sight of a signpost for Huy, one of the key points on the professional course, but fortunately we are spared this detour, with its severe climb reaching gradients of 25%. Our course is difficult enough as it is. In Ocquier (72km) we finally reach the first checkpoint at a small café in a narrow street of melancholy grey stone houses. The fields and crops give way to meadows and forests. Every descent is followed by another climb, mostly at around 6%, but the way up to the Côte de Warre (83km) involves a 10% climb.

In Bomal (89km) we reach a larger town for the first time, crossing bumpy railway lines and then the River Ourthe, followed immediately by the Aisne, whose level course we follow for the next three kilometres. It is worth mentioning, for, apart from the opening kilometres, this is the longest level stretch since starting out and there are not many more to come. Soon we are climbing again, this time 1.5 kilometres at 10%, to the Côte de Roche in Frene (100km), but it soon feels like 20%.

At the top there is a feed station: a muesli bar and an apple are provided, and water bottles can be refilled. Our race cards are not required here but they are studied carefully by many riders at this point, as they contain valuable information about villages, and distances of climbs are also detailed.

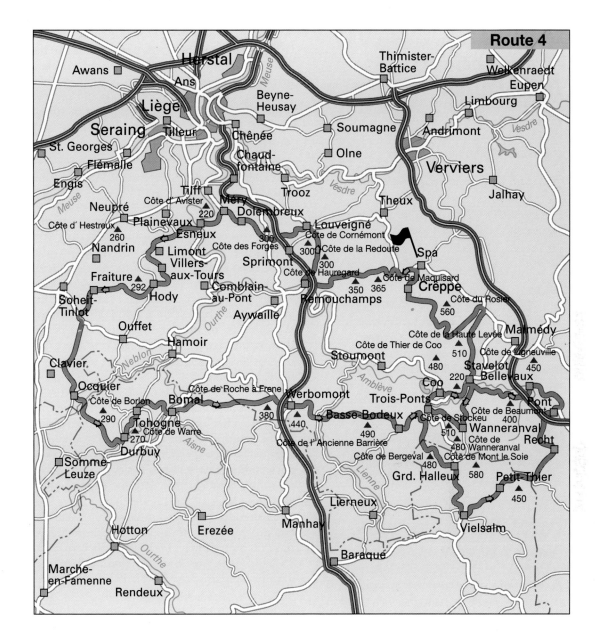

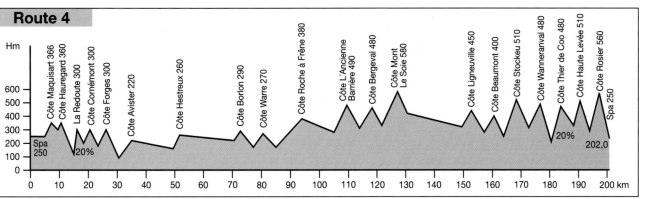

Organisational Information

Date – Early May

Distance – 202km and 114km

Total hill climbs – 3220 and 2270 metres

Highest climb – 20% on a 300 metre section of the Côte de la Redoute, and for about 300 metres on the Côte de Thier de Coo

Gearing – 42x26/28

Start place – Spa, reached from the Aachen motorway from Spa/Treves/Verviers exit, then leave the E42 at exit 8 (Spa). Turn sharp left immediately after entering the town, and follow the signs for 'La Fraineuse'. The Centre Sportif La Fraineuse is situated about 1km outside Spa

Accommodation – Hotels and campsite in Spa

Start time – Appointed start times between 5am and 8am

Entry fee – 150 Belgian francs

Feed stations – A muesli bar, an apple and drinks are available from one feed station

Participants – About 1500

Contact address – Cyclo Spa, 47 Rue Albin Body, B-4900 Spa, or, Cyclo Spa, Bte Postale 66, B-4900 Spa, Belgium

There are still 10 ahead of us, two of these are three kilometres long with 6% gradients, before the next checkpoint on the Côte de Bergeval (125km), where drinks and cakes can be bought.

We have long since stopped counting the climbs. They are not signposted and are as ordinary as the villages, with their uniform brickwork, and churches with steep gothic steeples. The gradient is mostly about 6%, sometimes the climbs are longer, sometimes shorter, but then a steeper section of 700 metres at 12% looms up before we reach Stavelot (160km). Down in the valley, the village with its extensive monastery and grounds lies enticingly before us, and the descent would be so tempting, but we must take care. Too late do we catch sight of the arrows directing us on to the side-road, our brakes are applied at the last moment, but there is no chance of choosing the right gear for the immediate 14% climb, and struggling on in the wrong gear is impossible, for the gradient continues for a good 300 metres. We have to dismount to engage the right gear, before continuing the climb to the Côte de Stockeu at a slightly easier but still agonising rate of climb.

We have rarely longed so much for a descent, but before that, the torture ends at the third checkpoint (163.5km). The subsequent one kilometre descent is banned for support vehicles. The course is too narrow here, and at 12% extremely steep. The corresponding climb to the Côte de Wanneranval (167km) awaits us. If the idea hasn't occurred to us already, we will soon be wishing that we had an emergency 28 tooth sprocket to tackle this 500 metre long 11% climb, which reaches 13% on the two hairpin bends. For the mainly Belgian and Dutch riders that I've met here, a 23 sprocket seems to be the largest that their bikes are equipped with, it seems barely adequate, for the gradient steadily gets worse, particularly on the Côte de Thier de Coo (177km). The 1.5 kilometre climb starts at 10%, gets steeper and steeper, finally reaching 20% for the last 300 metres. Drinks offered at a feed station are gladly received before the climb continues at 8%.

Then we roll on down to Stavelot (180km), a disappointingly short respite of 300 metres, and soon we are climbing again, this time at 8% for some distance to the top of the Côte de la Haute Levée (188km). Another two kilometres at 6% brings us up to the Côte du Rosier (196km), and we've done

The exceptionally fine weather during this Belgian classic raised the spirits of these riders

it at last. Now there is an almost continuous descent into Spa (200km), and at the finishing line (202km) we can be truly proud of our achievement, but many might think that a 202 kilometre ride with total hill climb of 3220 metres is a little excessive at the beginning of May.

Amstel Gold (Dwars door Limburg)   5
Holland

Windmills like this one look so typical of Holland, but they are quite rare in the province of Limburg

*D*wars-door Limburg means, literally, criss-crossing Limburg and is the name of the tourist's ride over the course of the best-known Dutch professional classic: the Amstel Gold.

More than half the land mass of Holland is below sea level and is considered flat. The southernmost province of Limburg, wedged between Belgium and Germany, is the exception, for the hilliest parts of Holland are located here in the foothills of the Ardennes with altitudes of around 200 metres. For this reason riders will find the climbs more difficult than they anticipate.

There is a vast sport and recreation centre in Glanerbrook, Geleen, which marks the start of the race for enthusiastic cyclists. It has a wide range of facilities, and in the month of August cyclists can ride in an organised event which begins at the roller skating rink. We depart in groups at five-minute intervals. The route is marked out by yellow signs with black arrows, usually fixed to lampposts and other street signs, but they can be difficult to spot.

The immaculately kept town is soon left behind and the countryside opens up. Green meadows, the odd tree and occasional industrial site come into view – the northern part of Limburg is as flat as a board!

Despite the five-minute interval between groups, after the start some groups split and others merge to ride in one another's slipstream. In no time at all there is a field of 100 riders which takes up the entire width of the road. Some hot-shots set a pace that gives a real race atmosphere. Others are cautious – the course is long and the climbs are still to come.

The first short climb is in Berg (36km) it is 200-metres long with a 6% gradient. The group is still intact and comes to the first checkpoint in Stein, at the Café t'Vesjke with 41.5 kilometres showing on the odometer. The fact that the café is only six kilometres from Limburg illustrates the notion of the route criss-crossing Limbourg.

The course continues to unfold with a short descent of around 12% but over cobblestones. Then there is a short stretch alongside the Juliana Canal and after a narrow underpass comes another climb of nearly a kilometre at 6%, ending abruptly at the stop sign of a crossroads. The next landmark, at the side of the road, is the first and only windmill on the course. The southern part of Limburg is not the land of dykes and canals, windmills and watermills. It is agricultural land of rolling hills and dales in which state-of-the-art farming technology is practised. Following the contours of the landscape, the road rolls on, but it is not until after the Valkenburg (15km) that riders reach the next climb.

The Café Conemans in Ubachsberg (85.5km) is the next checkpoint and our pause here will be surely somewhat longer than the first! When we resume the course we notice a marked change in the landscape, it is clearly more hilly and riders tackle climbs of 8% and about a kilometre long. Before Gulpen there is a slight chicane – a 500-metre climb steep enough to tax most riders with its 12% gradient. Over the top of the hill some of us get to enjoy the view in the shade of the trees, then swooping down the road we have to brake sharply at the first row of houses in Gulpen (107km)

The rolling roads continue into Epen (115.5km) and a three-kilometre climb up a 9% gradient. It is a climb marked on the maps as being 212 metres above sea level. At the Restaurant Blutenlust (118.5km) just below the highest point, there is confusion – one road goes straight on and another branches to the left. There is no signpost to be seen, and the otherwise excellent route map, given to the participants, is also of no help! Both roads lead to the next checkpoint in Vijlen (122.5km), but those who branched off to the left saved themselves about five kilometres along a hillier road. In the Café Aan de Boom we pause for lunch, after which we resume the second half of the tour. Neither the landscape nor the course profile changes: climbs of up to 10%, followed by quick descents and lengthy flat sections. Small hills and dales punctuate the route, villages and towns rapidly succeed each other for Holland is one of the most densely populated countries in the world.

In Meerssen (167km) there is another surprise: by a railway embankment an arrow points to the right, whilst another sign points straight on. The solution to the puzzle is not to turn off to the right towards Geultal for

Route 5

those who do will go in circles for a good 60 kilometres ending back at the same point.

The fourth checkpoint is the Café Geulhemermolen (171km) and a fierce 600-metre climb taking us out of the valley – forcing some to dismount and walk. There follows further climbs, descents and villages leading to Keutenberg Street in Strucht (185.5km). It is described in our brochure as a hill, this may seem inaccurate to riders struggling up its 22% gradient, but they'll have little time to think about it on the 50 metre slope. The next 200 metres reduce the gradient slightly to 18% and it eases once again to 12% before reaching the summit, marked Keutenberg. Usually some spectators gather here to encourage riders. Most dismount and walk, but a few are able to climb using a big gear. The die-hards will insist on fighting it out with their last ounce of strength and a gear of 42x21.

After the summit there are pastoral scenes to enjoy: farmyards, meadows and fields full of cows, then down the 18% descent to Stockhem (188.5km). Afterwards the hilly landscape from Eys (193.5km) and its longish climbs of 8% will seem tame after the Keutenberg. Riders pass the town sign of Valkenberg twice after several dips and dales to arrive back in Meerssen (230.5km). Once the railway is crossed the difficult parts of the course are over and the road is mostly flat when the Geleen sign comes into view (238km), eventually turning back towards the roller-rink in Glanerbrook to complete the 242 kilometres.

Riders approach the second checkpoint in the café Conemans in Ubachuberg after 85.5 kilometres

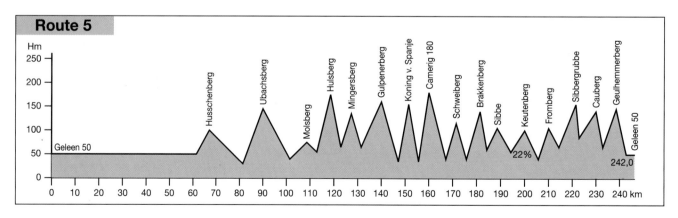

Organisational Information

Date – Mid August

Distance – 242 kilometres

Total hill climbs – Approximately 2000 metres

Highest climb – The Keutenberg, 500 metres long, 50 metres at 22% 200 metres at 18% and the rest is 12%. Many climbs are up to 12% and 600-metres long

Gearing – 42x26/28

Start place – Glanerbrook sportpark in Geleen. From Aachen on the motorway take the Geleen exit. Follow the main road towards the town, turn right from Kummenaedestraat to the stadium

Accommodation – Hotels in Geleen. There is a low-cost campsite with all facilities within the stadium

Start time – Appointed start times between 6am and 9am

Entry fee – Approximately 7.50 Dutch gilders

Feed stations – There are no official feed stations, however in most villages there are cafés and shops where refreshments can be obtained

Participants – About 3000

Contact address – Wielerclub De Ster Geleen, c/o Dhr M Meuders, Op de Vey 15, 6165 CA Geleen, Netherlands

Further Information – An early departure is recommended to avoid heavy traffic that builds up around mid-day

This view of the Keutenberg shows riders tackling the 22% gradient in their own style

Tour
of Flanders
Belgium

6

A lone rider attacks the 12% cobbled climb of the Kwaremont

*A*t six o'clock in the morning in mid-August it is still dark in East Flanders. Yet at this dark hour about 200 cyclists gather outside the little Café 't Molenhuis in St Martens-Latem (0.0km). There will be closer to 500 or 600 cyclists by 8am as that is the official start time. All of these riders are about to take on the 223 kilometres of the *Trofee Karel van Wijnendaele*, of which a good 130 kilometres follow the original route of the professional Tour of Flanders classic.

There is no organised start, just a stamp on the race card, the first rider sets out, and others follow. No one has lights, but at this time of day there are no cars to be seen. In Huise (24km) we join the professional route; the starting point is situated in St. Niklaas, near Antwerp. Gradually the day dawns, and a morning mist hangs over the roadside meadows, where the vague outlines of black and white cows can be made out. A few windmills loom dark, with their long, almost ghostly sails, and in the east the sun rises like a glowing red ball. These are impressions which remain in the memory from the first few, level kilometres. But there is something else that is just as unforgettable the cobblestone surface, which we come across for the first time after 20 kilometres. After only a few metres there is only one way to describe it – terrible!

These thoroughfares can hardly be called roads, especially when one's mode of transport is a bicycle, and inevitably the first mechanical problems occur. Some riders move over on to the narrow strip of earth between the road and the maize fields in an effort to escape the shake up. Originally, these were just farm paths through the fields, paved with cobblestones to a width of about three metres, the surface has a marked convex profile to enable the rainwater to run away. This precaution was hardly necessary, however, since the one or two centimetre gaps between the stones provides plenty of space for the water to soak into the earth beneath. To a cyclist each of these gaps

Even the professionals struggle up these short, steep cobblestone climbs

Organisational Information

Date – Mid August

Distance – 223 kilometres

Total hill climbs – Approximately 1200 metres

Highest climb – 20% for about 100 metres on the Patersberg. 18% for about 200 metres on the Muur in Geraardsbergen, 15 other short climbs between 10% and 16%

Gearing – 42x26/28

Start Place – St Martens-Latem to the west of Ghent, can be reached from motorway exit 14 (Deinze) if approaching from Brussels. Starting point is the Café 't Molenhuis, Maenhoutstraat 78, and is signposted with small yellow and white placards bearing the wording 'Het Nieuwsblad/Trofee karel van Wijnendaele'

Accommodation – Hotels in St Martens-Latem. There is a low-cost campsite in a small field close to the start line, but it does not have full facilities

Start time – Appointed start times between 6am and 8am

Entry fee – 100 Belgian francs

Feeding – A waffle and two cans of lemonade are distributed at one of the checkpoints

Participants – About 800

Contact address – V C Karel van Wijnendaele, c/o Pennoit Willy, Steengoedstraat 3, B-9910 Ghent or V C Karel van Wijnendaele-Hertekamp, c/o Gerhard D'Heere, Hofakkerlaan 17, B-9052 Zwijnaarde, Belgium

Further information – The greater part of the course follows almost traffic free side-roads and is route marked on the road surface with three yellow arrows. The tortuous nature of the route makes it advisable to stay in contact with riders who have local knowledge. A cobblestone surace covers about 10km of the course

means a jolt transmitted to the body through tyre and wheel rim with no suspension to reduce the effect.

However hard one tries it is not possible to reach a reasonable speed. The handlebars must be gripped tightly, preferably on the top bar. It is impossible to take away one hand to change gear or use the brakes. Soon your forearms and fingers begin to ache. Thankfully, after almost three kilometres this section is finally at an end. In Eine (27.5km) we cross the Schelde, Belgium's greatest river, and we approach Molenberg (36.5km) travelling on side-roads, where we tackle the first climb, or 'hell', as the locals would say.

A line of houses leaves some room for a narrow cobbled lane, which leads up to a small hilltop over a distance of 300 metres at 12%. In Horebeke (41.5km) we are faced with another three kilometres of cobblestones, but at the first checkpoint at the Café Breughel in Ename (51.5km) we can fortify ourselves with a black coffee. The going is level now, the road sign for Ronse comes into view and brings back memories of the 1988 World Championships, when Steve Bauer brought down the Flemish rider Claude Criquielion in the final sprint. We do not reach Ronse itself, but perhaps the championship route covered one of the roads we are travelling today. They all look much the same: concrete surfaces with expansion gaps, countless cracks and innumerable repairs. There are hardly any cobblestones ahead, just a few short sections, which should pose no problems, but the remaining climbs are a different matter.

In Kwaremont (70km) there is another 'hell', almost 800 metres long: 500 metres of its length are cobbled, and have a 12% gradient. Shortly afterwards comes the Patersberg, starting easily, but then, on rounding a bend, it suddenly rises like the side of a house at 20%. Many riders struggle up this 100 metre section standing on the pedals and using 42x26 gearing, whilst others conquer the hill in the saddle with a triple chainwheel and 28x28 gearing. Before the next checkpoint at the Café 'Hof der Vlaamse Ardennen' (100km) there are another four of these 'killer' climbs to negotiate. Of these, however, only the Taaienberg reaches 16%.

Now we reach rolling countryside with

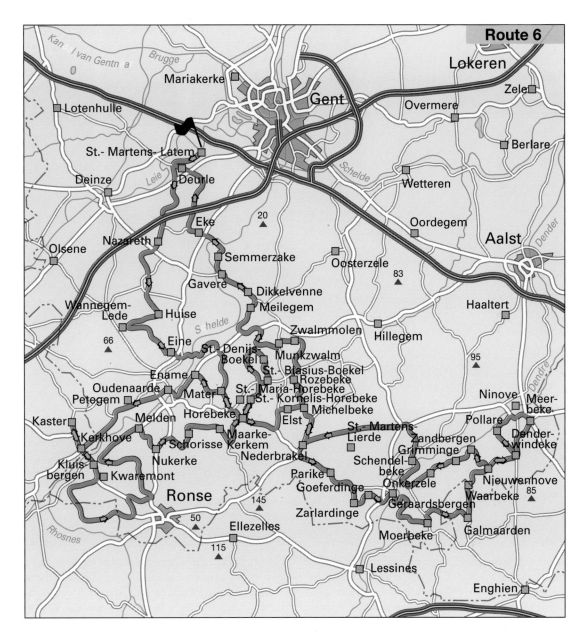

Route 6

Route 6

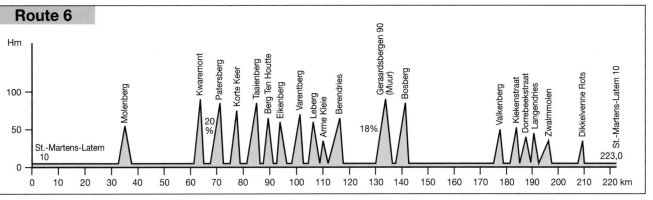

Hm

- St.-Martens-Latem 10
- Molenberg
- Kwaremont
- 20%
- Patersberg
- Korte Keer
- Taaienberg
- Berg Ten Houtte
- Eikenberg
- Varentberg
- Leberg
- Arme Kleie
- Berendries
- Geraardsbergen 90 (Muur)
- 18%
- Bosberg
- Valkenberg
- Kiekenstraat
- Dorrebeekstraat
- Langendries
- Zwalmmolen
- Dikkelvenne Rots
- St.-Martens-Latem 10
- 223,0

0 10 20 30 40 50 60 70 80 90 100 110 120 130 140 150 160 170 180 190 200 210 220 km

short climbs, mostly under 10%, alternating with descents and long level stretches. Inevitably we are approaching Geraardsbergen (129km) with its infamous Muur – the wall. Shortly after crossing the Dender it lies before us and can hardly be overlooked, with its white 'Muur' inscribed on the road surface. The 12% climb between the brick-built houses, branches off after 600 metres into a side street, we are on the cobblestones again, and the gradient increases to 18% for almost 200 metres. At the top we come across an additional and completely unexpected checkpoint, and then there are no more difficulties before we reach the next official checkpoint at the Café 'Onder De Linde' in Meerbeke (147.5km). The professional race ends here in Meerbeke, but we continue on twisting side-roads in the Geraardsbergen area, and only twice are we forced into greater efforts by short climbs of up to 12%.

In Michelbeke (182.5km) we reach the last checkpoint, from which a 9% climb of about one kilometre takes us into the final section. A fairly easy undulating road follows, and only in Backer-Stemme (202km) is there a short 100 metre climb with a gradient of 12%. The last kilometres are flat as a board, leading us back to the little Café 't Molenhuis (223km) through shady avenues and residential streets with their 'sleeping policemen'. At the end of the ride there is no great commotion here, riders gather in small groups, some of them will sit together in the café, but the majority soon head for home.

Punctures are always a possibility on the roads of Flanders. These two riders seem to be a well-practised team

Milan– San Remo

Italy

Tropical vegetation, a mild climate and fine weather make even 290 kilometres of cycling seem a pleasure

*M*ilan still sleeps as the start time approaches, but by the Luigi Carraro Sports Centre on the southern outskirts of the city there is lively activity. Buses and vans are unloading varied groups of cyclists from Holland, Belgium, Germany, Switzerland, France and, of course, Italy. The floodlights of the football pitch and the street lamps provide enough light for final preparations before the start, and then we have to queue to have our race cards stamped in the foyer of the sports centre. Singly or in groups the first riders set out on their long journey, and are soon swallowed up by the darkness. Only a few riders have lights on their bikes; a rear light would be very advisable. Admittedly there is little traffic on the roads, but now and again a car speeds past out of the darkness, its occupants probably intent on using the early morning *houra* for a Sunday hunting expedition. It therefore seems safer to join one of the numerous club groups, which are nearly always protected by one or more support vehicles.

Not until we have left Pavia (25km) after an hour's ride does the darkness begin to give way to the dawn, but for a long time a heavy ground mist over the surrounding fields holds back any real daylight. We ride unnoticed through small, still sleeping villages, and there is a ghostly effect when, in the diffuse light of the street lamps, we are overtaken by our own shadows, which grow ever bigger, only to disappear in an instant. Ahead, the lead groups maintain a brisk tempo. There are always a few people at the front riding as if the finishing line were in the next village, but on these totally flat roads even the slower riders find it easy to keep up. The first 100 kilometres and more are so flat that the short, easy gradient leading up to the bridge over the Po (38km) is the first noticeable climb.

Around Silvana d' Orba (112km) we see a range of hills rising ahead, they are the lower slopes of the Ligurian Alps, which separate the Plain of Lombardy from the Mediterranean. Although the road remains flat, the scenery changes, and the fields and pastures give way to leafy, mixed woodland. After Ovada (124km) a first easy climb takes us below the motorway into a thickly wooded valley. At Gnocchetto (129km) we leave Piedmont for Liguria and a sign indicates that the summit of the Turchino Pass is still 16 kilometres away.

The highest point of the tour is at 532 metres; we have already ridden about 250 metres, and so the remaining 280 metres of altitude are covered easily. Gradients which rarely exceed 4% are relieved by long level stretches, and it is only in the last two kilometres before the tunnel, at the summit (146km), that the gradient reaches a regular 5%. Anyone who is not well up at the head of the field will cover the last part of the climb amongst a line of support vehicles, which finally form a traffic jam at the entrance to the 150 metre tunnel, and for which there is far too little space available at the tunnel exit, where the first checkpoint is situated.

A little more than 10 kilometres of sweeping descent with a few hairpin bends now await us, and this ends on the outskirts of Genoa (158km), only a stone's throw from the sea. We follow the Via Aurelia, the B1, which runs along the Riviera di Ponente, as this stretch of coast is called. Shortly after Geneva at Arenzano the road leads inland, climbing gently for about two kilometres and dropping back immediately to the coast. The narrow coastal strip is densely populated, and so we ride through townships of varying size, where the rocky coastline is sometimes broken by sandy seaside promenades. The road is level with a slight gradient now and again, but rarely anything exceeding 5%. Such climbs are rare, however, as are the few tunnels along this section, posing no threat to our progress.

Despite it being like the rush hour on a Sunday afternoon, the heavy traffic on this stretch does not seem to hinder us, so preoccupied are we with riding and admiring the landscape around us. If a larger group forms it will move along with no difficulty, for on the sweeping bends, few cars are able to overtake the throng of support vehicles. Such a group is not held up by red lights, since the traffic police here are on the side of the cyclists. Care is still required, however, since the riding style of many competitors is much too high spirited. Suddenly someone will kick out at a companion, throw his arms in the air in a victory salute on passing a village boundary sign, and riding over a manhole cover can cause as much uproar as a pretty girl by the roadside.

In Vado Ligure, after 191 kilometres, we reach the only feed station. An apple, mineral water, biscuits, jam, a bread roll, and a carton of fruit juice are supplied in a feeding bag, too little, admittedly, for this distance, but nevertheless a nice gesture from the organisers, which is gratefully accepted. The finishing line still seems a long way off, but strangely fatigue is not a problem, hardly any riders are have trouble with the course and there is no need to point out to anyone the distance already covered. The mild climate, the sea, the palms and agaves, the almost flat course, and not least the motivation which comes from riding in the last highlight of the season with like-minded companions: all of these things seem to combine to lend us wings.

In Laiuéglia (243km), however, many are brought back to earth as the road climbs up from the sea three times in succession. These climbs are about 1.5 kilometres in length with gradients up to 6%. and the last one to the Capo Berta (257.5km) increases to 8%. By now our legs are feeling the effects of the kilometres, yet some race away as if there were a mountain 'prime' to be won, but at the top there's a long queue of cyclists waiting for the checkpoint marshal, who, hopelessly overstretched by the throng of riders, is stamping their cards calmly and unhurriedly. Now only the Poggio awaits us. We have heard and read far too much about this climb, which regularly plays the part of 'the executioner' in the professional event, to prevent ourselves from feeling a thrill of anticipation. The course continues on level ground, however, and in San Lorenzo (269km) a road branches off to the right towards the Cipressa, but we are spared the 5.5 kilometres with gradients of up to 7% and an altitude change of 250 metres, which is indeed part of the professional course.

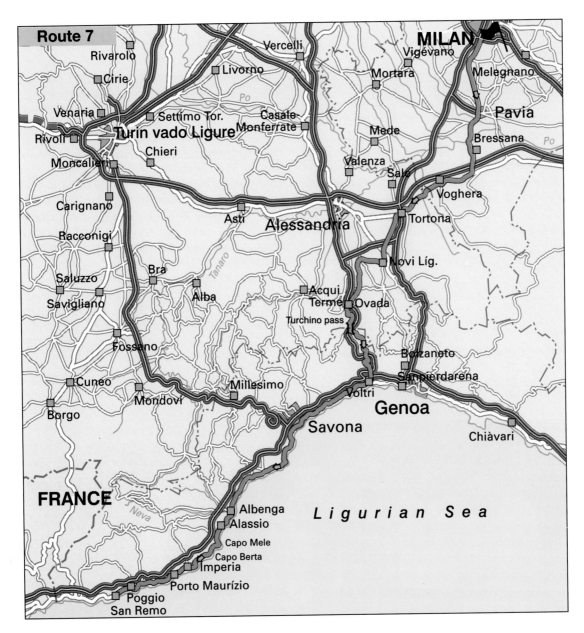

Route 7

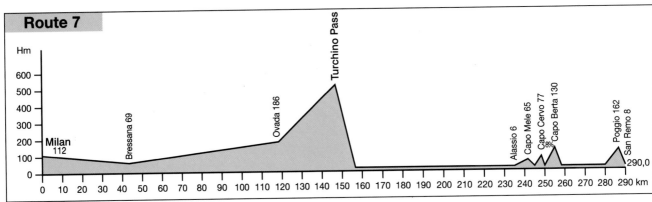

Organisational Information

Date – Mid September

Distance – 290 kilometres

Total hill climbs – 850 metres

Highest climb – Several hundred metres at 8% on the Capo Berta

Gearing – 42x21/23

Start place – Luigi Carraro sports centre, Via Missaglia 146, in Milan. The starting point is not signposted and so it is difficult to find. If approaching from the north, it is advisable to drive around the outskirts of Milan on the Tangente Ovest and to leave the motorway at the Viale Liguria exit. Then drive towards the town centre and watch out for signs to the Centro Sportivo Luigi Carraro'. It is advisable to take along a street map. As a rough guide, the sports centre is situated on the southern outskirts of Milan, immediately next to the boundary of Rozzano

Start time – Appointed start times between 6am and 7.15am

Entry fee – 20,000 lire

Feed stations – A feed bag is provided in Vado Ligure at around 191km

Participants – About 1500

Contact address – Unione Cicloturistica San Remo, c/o Bar Ciclosport, Corso Inglesi 294, 1-18038 San Remo (IM), Italy

Further information – This tour is undertaken for the most part by clubs and groups, but individual entrants are allowed to participate. According to the regulations participation is only open to members of cycling clubs or similar associations. Therefore, applications must be made through a club, that is, on the club's headed notepaper. For foreign riders the club must confirm that the member is covered by third party insurance. It appears, however, that exceptions to the 'members only' rule are made. It is advisable to contact the organisers in such cases. Telephone numbers can be found in the tour's detailed information booklet. No checks are made at the start in respect of licence, club identity card, head protection or lighting. With a 6am start a rear light is strongly recommended. Return transport from San Remo to Milan is not arranged by the organisers

The road continues on the level, San Remo is getting closer, as we can see from the road signs. We are almost on the outskirts of San Remo (282.5km) when we reach an inconspicuous road to the right, signposted with the word 'Poggio'. The road climbs for the next two kilometres at a regular 6%, with several hairpin bends, passing smallholdings, small vineyards with stone-built wells, greenhouses, stone walls and a great deal of sun scorched scrub. At the Hotel Belvedere the gradient eases, many riders take a rest, and look out far across the sea, but a short 7% climb follows a flat section before the road finally rises gently into the centre of the Poggio (286.5km). The last checkpoint is up there.

We ride round the hairpin bends down to San Remo, where a policeman is on duty at the entrance to the main street, and a marshal directs us into the Corsa Garibaldi, a very narrow poplar lined avenue. Suddenly we find ourselves in a roomy multi-storey car park (290km), we hand in our race cards, and receive a fine certificate and a drink, and the Milan–San Remo is over.

Europa Cup Marathons

The Europa Cup Marathons were inaugurated in 1987 in order to give cycling enthusiasts further incentive to take part in cycle touring events. Payment of a small licence fee entitles riders to take part in the events which make up the series, and also includes other concessions. For example: when starting their first event, Europa Cup riders receive a jersey bearing their personal start number, which identifies them as Europa Cup competitors. They are also entitled to start at the front of any massed start, and after each event they receive an additional gift. If in the course of the year the rider successfully completes at least three of the planned events (currently six events per year), a certificate and an award will be presented. Any rider can be proud of these, for the awards are not easily obtained. As a quick look at any route plan will show: an incredible altitude change of 5000 metres over 185 kilometres in the Dolomite Marathon or even the altitude change of 5500 metres over 229 kilometres on the Ötztaler Marathon. Events can hardly come harder than these and the mere 3300 metres altitude difference over 250 kilometres of the Arber Marathon seem modest by comparison.

The Europa Cup is recognised as a challenge which makes considerable demands on the perseverance and endurance of its participants, whose numbers have been restricted to 500 every year. It is intended that the Europa Cup should be restricted to current events. Changes have already been made, however, because of a change of sponsor, for instance, or organisational difficulties, and so such alterations cannot be ruled out in the future. I have therefore described the five events which have been included in the Europa Cup calendar since its inception.

It should be emphasised that you can of course take part in the following events without being the holder of a Europa Cup licence. You are then not entitled to the special jersey, the right to start from the front row, nor the additional award. Participation in the traditional Europa Cup party on the eve of the event, is, of course, restricted to licence holders.

Further information about Europa Cup Marathons can be obtained from:

VCR-Regensburg
EC-Organisations-Komitee
Pflanzenmayerstrasse 8a
8400 Regensburg
Germany

Note: In 1990, the Cycle Touring Super Cup was introduced for the first time. In contrast to the Europa Cup, these events, seven in number, are routed within the borders of Germany, and require perseverance and endurance. The shortest distance is 200 kilometres, the maximum 325 kilometres, and the total hill climb figure can amount to more than 3000 metres. Basically, anyone may take part in the events, but only members of the German Cycling Federation who hold a valid competition licence are considered for the Super Cup Classification, which again involves special awards. The programme for the Super Cup Series can be obtained on receipt of a stamped addressed envelope from:

Bund Deutscher Radfahrer
Otto-Fleck-Schneise 4
6000 Frankfurt/Main
Germany

You can also obtain information about possible membership of the BDR from the same address.

Schneeberg–Wechsel Marathon *8*

Austria

These three riders on the climb to the Ascher Pass have opened up a small lead on the pursuing field, 40 kilometres into the race

What do Eddy Merckx, arguably the most successful cyclist of all time, and World Rally Champion Walter Röhrl have in common? Both of them have ridden in the Schneeberg-Wechsel Marathon. According to reports they are said to have been deeply impressed. The course is, in fact, very demanding, and the organisers are at pains to do justice to their reputation for being responsible for 'the most professional touring event of the Europa Cup', and the best Austrian touring event.

It's no wonder that the event is becoming ever more popular, and that the field of almost 2000 riders gathered in the narrow main street of Kirchberg am Wechsel stretches back to the town boundary. Right at the front of the field are the riders who took part in the Mountain Time Trial, held the

day before, they are Europa Cup licence holders. Any one of whom would be pleased to take home the mountain bike offered this year as the prize for the rider with the fastest time over the long course. The start is on time at 7am, and there is no time for a warm-up, for the first climb to the Ramssattel begins after 400 metres, even before the village has been left behind.

The road climbs for four kilometres at a regular gradient of between 6% and 8% through dense forest, and the first riders have already reached the first summit at the Gasthof Ramswirt (5km), as the last are just attacking the first hairpin bend on the lower third of the climb. From this summit the road continues to climb at 6% for another 500 metres before falling away to open up views

The 14% climb to the Pfaffensattel after 248 hard kilometres really calls for an all-out effort

Organisational Information

Date – Mid June

Distance – 248, 185 and 120 kilometres

Total hill climbs – 3490, 2660 and 1340 metres

Highest climb – 2 kilometres at 14% on the Pfaffensattel

Gearing – 42x26

Start place – Kirchberg am Wechsel, approx 50km southwest of Wiener Neustadt

Accommodation – Hotels in and around Kirchberg

Start time – Massed start at 7am

Entry fee – 350 Austrian schillings (approx)

Feed stations – There are 5 feed stations

Participants – About 2000

Contact address – Radclub Drahtesel, Kirchberg am Wechsel, A-2880 Kirchberg, Austria

across the wooded hillsides of the 'Bucklige Welt' – literally meaning Roller-Coaster Land – as the landscape between Semmering and the Wechsel Pass is known. Sweeping down through wide curves and small villages to the broad floor of the Schwarza Valley, the road continues on the level as far as Ternitz (19km).

A police motor cycle escorts the leading group and ensures free passage for them, whilst a loudspeaker hails from the organisers car informing the few onlookers at the roadside that an international cycling event is taking place. Beyond Sieding (25.5km) we ride through a narrow archway into the Sierning Valley, but we still do not need to use the small chainwheel yet, for the almost level road to Puchberg (33.5km) is only interrupted by a short 100 metre climb at around 6%. The Schneeberg, one of the mountains after which the event is named, comes into view. This 2000 metre mountain, with its long barren summit ridge, is still capped with the last remains of winter snow, even in the middle of June. On the outskirts of Puchberg, however, it is necessary to reach for the gear lever, as the road climbs up to the Ascher Pass (40km) at 8% for a good two kilometres. The subsequent descent is hardly any longer than the climb, and the gradient is no steeper than that of the ascent. The danger comes, in fact, from the support vehicles, which keep pushing their way through between the riders.

The route is completely flat to Reichental (48km), and even as far as Gutenstein (59km) there are hardly any climbs. We have time enough to recover, but anyone who has joined a fast group must use all of his strength if he is to stay in the slipstream. The first feed station is at the entrance to the Kloster Valley (66km), and feeling refreshed, we attack the third climb of the day. For the first five kilometres the large chainwheel can be used, and then the gradient increases to 6%, only to steepen again to 8% on the last 1.5 kilometres up to the summit. There is a short descent and we turn into the Höllental (Hell Valley), where the Schwarza has cut its way between the brooding, craggy and precipitous rock-faces. At Hirschwang (93km) we have covered the wild, romantic part of the route, and the road continues levelly as far as Prein an der Rax (101km).

Even the five kilometre long climb to the Preiner-Gschaid Pass is not actually difficult: the gradient remains mostly at 6%, and only increases to 11% in two places. By now, in the shadow of the Rax range, the kilometres already covered make themselves felt. A stop at the feed station on the pass summit (106km) is usually avoided by most riders, they prefer to press on, and for the next 25 kilometres to Spital (131km) there are no troublesome gradients.

This soon changes, even though riders may hesitate to engage the small chainwheel on entering the Fröschnitz Valley because of the moderate gradient, it becomes unavoidable at the first hairpin bend (141km). The gradient increases gradually to 10% as further hairpins are encountered. This is not the

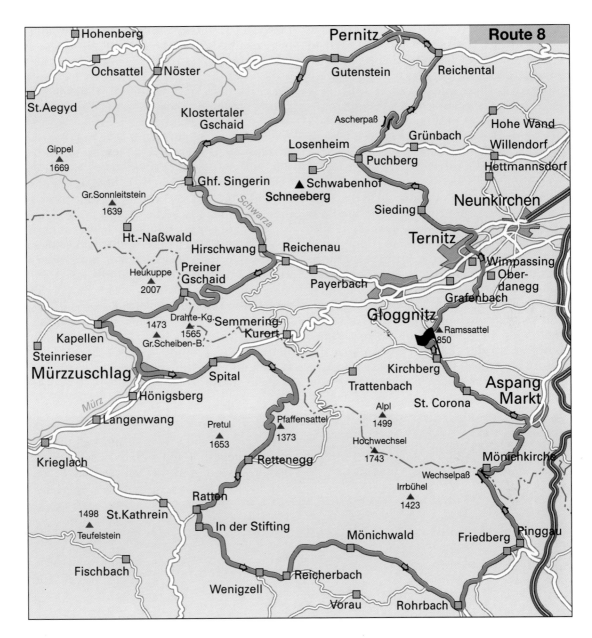

Route 8

Hohenberg
Ochsattel   Nöster
St.Aegyd
                          Klostertaler
                          Gschaid
Gippel
1669
                          Ghf. Singerin
Gr.Sonnleitstein
1639
Ht.-Naßwald
Heukuppe   Preiner
2007   Gschaid
                  Drahte-Kg.
              1473   1565   Semmering-
Kapellen   Gr.Scheiben-B.   Kurort
Steinrieser
Mürzzuschlag
              Hönigsberg   Spital
              Langenwang
Krieglach   Pretul
                       1653   Pfaffensattel
                                    1373
                            Rettenegg
              Ratten
1498 St.Kathrein
Teufelstein   In der Stifting
Fischbach
                  Wenigzell   Reicherbach
                       Vorau   Rohrbach

Pernitz
Gutenstein   Reichental
                  Ascherpaß
              Losenheim   Grünbach   Hohe Wand
                                        Willendorf
                  Puchberg   Hettmannsdorf
              Schwabenhof
Schneeberg   Sieding   Neunkirchen
              Ternitz
Hirschwang   Reichenau   Wimpassing
                                Ober-
              Payerbach   danegg
                        Grafenbach
                  Gloggnitz
                        Ramssattel
                        850
              Kirchberg
              Trattenbach   Aspang
              St. Corona   Markt
         Alpl
         1499
    Hochwechsel   Mönichkirche
    1743
              Wechselpaß
         Irrbühel
         1423
                                Pinggau
              Mönichwald   Friedberg

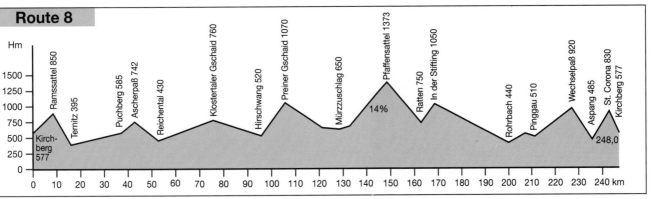

Route 8

Hm

1500
1250
1000
750
500
250
0

Kirch-
berg
577

Ramssattel 850

Ternitz 395

Puchberg 585
Ascherpaß 742

Reichental 430

Klostertaler Gschaid 760

Hirschwang 520

Preiner Gschaid 1070

Mürzzuschlag 650

Pfaffensattel 1373

14%

Ratten 750
In der Stifting 1050

Rohrbach 440

Pinggau 510

Wechselpaß 920

Aspang 485
St. Corona 830
Kirchberg 577

248,0

0 10 20 30 40 50 60 70 80 90 100 110 120 130 140 150 160 170 180 190 200 210 220 230 240 km

whole story, however, for the course rises like a ramp to 14% and stays steep all the way to the summit, which for two kilometres seems to last an eternity. The spectators who have gathered up here encourage us with their applause, but the immediate descent, signposted as having gradients of up to 20%, must be tackled with great care, even though the actual gradient does not exceed 16%.

There is very little space up here at the top of the Pfaffensattel pass, and so we must ride down to the feed station at Rettenegg (156km), where the routes of the medium length and long courses separate. Whilst those on the former route are 'only' faced with the 10% climb to the Feistritzsattel with its altitude of 400 metres, three more difficult climbs await those on the latter. The first climb immediately after Ratten (165km) is a good two kilometres in length and has a gradient of up to 12%, leading up to a ridge known as 'In der Stifting', from which the road to Rohrbach an der Lafnitz (200km) again drops away gently. The next section of rolling countryside comes to a sudden end in Pinggau (211km), when the gradient increases to 12% at the start of the Wechsel Pass. Cobblestones present an additional difficulty over the next 1.5 kilometres, but then the climb eases and the slight gradients are evenly broken by short descents on our way to the summit (226km).

The last climb from Aspang Markt (234km) up to St Corona (242km) is not difficult, but, on the other hand, it is quite long. On its upper sections short, steeper climbs are encountered several times, but mostly these do not exceed 6%, and for long stretches are considerably less. From up here we catch our last glimpse of the Schneeberg, far away to the northwest, but most riders will find the view of Kirchberg far down below much more attractive. The route is all downhill to the finish (248km) – or is it? We have forgotten one last climb: in Kirchberg the road rises once again at 11% for 250 metres to the finishing line. But that can easily be ignored at this stage; we are so pleased to see the finish.

Swabian Alb extrem Marathon — 9
Germany

*T*he Swabian Alb has hosted a very challenging event over a very attractive route since 1984. The *extrem* description seems well justified because of its 225 kilometres and a total hill climb figure of 4400 metres, but there's a shorter route of 175 kilometres and 2800 metres of hill climb that is still long enough to be a challenge. Starting out from Ottenbach, the route passes through a charming range of hills between the upper Neckar and the Danube. Even the majority of Germans native to this region seem unaware that this is one of the most extensive continuous limestone landscapes in central Europe. The distinctive geological peculiarities of the area and the outstanding organisation of the event, fulfil all of the requirements to make this tour a memorable experience.

At five o clock in the morning there is lively activity around the starting area, and after registering our start time on our race cards by means of computer, we are on our way. After only a few kilometres the first climb begins on the outskirts of the town, taking us up the rounded, heavily wooded Kaiserberg Hohenstaufen, which dominates the immediate landscape. The gradient is signposted as 15%, and for this section, on a side road, closed to other traffic, the gradient applies to only a few metres if at all. Such a slow section will be welcome to many riders in the cool morning air. Beyond the village of Hohenstaufen we have to use the brakes, after a short descent, in order to turn on to an asphalt track, which brings us down a gentle slope to the first checkpoint (33km). Still full of energy, we look forward to the climb up the specially signposted 'Staufer Road' which passes some sites of local historical significance. Whether the packed car park at the starting area, which surprisingly can be seen clearly from up here, will also take its place in history is rather doubtful..

The charming landscape of the Swabian Alb is extremely inviting to keen cyclists

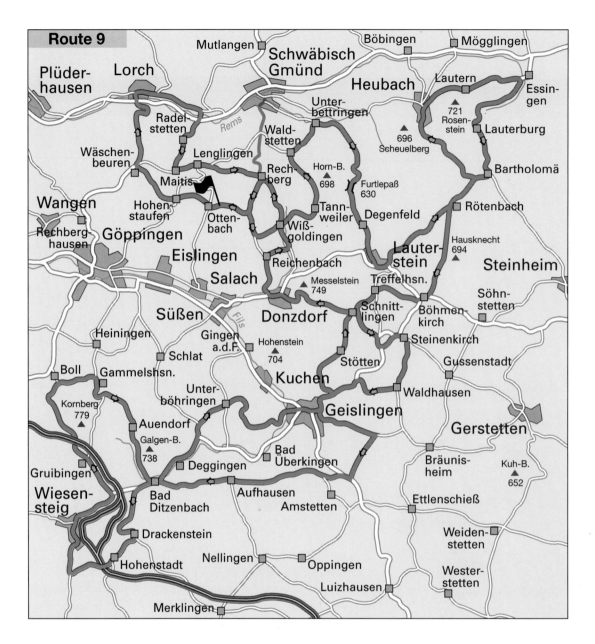

Route 9

Plüder-hausen
Lorch
Mutlangen
Schwäbisch Gmünd
Böbingen
Mögglingen
Heubach
Lautern
Essin-gen
Radel-stetten
Rems
Unter-bettringen
Rosen-stein 721
Lauterburg
Wäschen-beuren
Lenglingen
Wald-stetten
Rech-berg
Horn-B. 698
Scheuelberg 696
Furtlepaß 630
Bartholomä
Maitis
Hohen-staufen
Otten-bach
Tann-weiler
Degenfeld
Rötenbach
Wangen
Wiß-goldingen
Hausknecht 694
Rechberg-hausen
Göppingen
Reichenbach
Lauter-stein
Steinheim
Eislingen
Messelstein 749
Treffelhsn.
Söhn-stetten
Salach
Donzdorf
Schnitt-lingen
Böhmen-kirch
Süßen
Hohenstein 704
Steinenkirch
Heiningen
Gingen a.d.F.
Stötten
Gussenstadt
Schlat
Kuchen
Boll
Gammelshsn.
Unter-böhringen
Geislingen
Waldhausen
Kornberg 779
Auendorf
Gerstetten
Galgen-B. 738
Bad Überkingen
Bräunis-heim
Kuh-B. 652
Gruibingen
Deggingen
Aufhausen
Amstetten
Ettlenschieß
Wiesen-steig
Bad Ditzenbach
Weiden-stetten
Drackenstein
Nellingen
Oppingen
Wester-stetten
Hohenstadt
Luizhausen
Merklingen
Fils

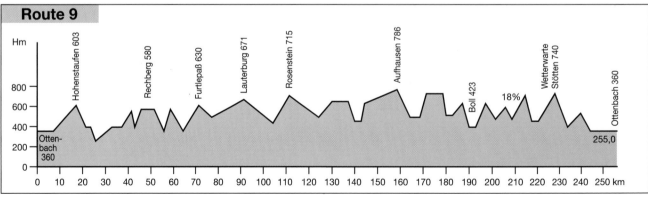

Route 9

Hm

Hohenstaufen 603

Rechberg 580

Furtlepaß 630

Lauterburg 671

Rosenstein 715

Aufhausen 786

Boll 423

18%

Wetterwarte Stötten 740

Ottenbach 360

Otten-bach 360

255,0

800
600
400
200
0

0 10 20 30 40 50 60 70 80 90 100 110 120 130 140 150 160 170 180 190 200 210 220 230 240 250 km

The road continues downhill, but then, on the next lengthy and relentless climb with its gradients of up to 12% (35km), we can tell who, amongst the riders, is a mountain specialist, a sprinter, or just a Sunday afternoon cyclist. Fortunately the course becomes rather less demanding after this, and the first feed station in Waldstetten (55km) is not far away. The roads are quite traffic free as we continue up to the Furtle Pass, encountering ascents of up to 10%, which are regularly interspersed with easy descents. Neither the degree of difficulty nor the surrounding scenery can persuade us to compare the climbs to those of the genuine Alpine passes.

After Degenfeld we ride up the Weissensteiner Steige, and continue on quiet side roads through sleepy villages, orchards and pasture land past the 721 metre Rosenstein – the massive mountain on the northern side of the Alb – finally reaching the second feed station in Lautern (85km). The next section which goes along the edge of the Heidenheimer Alb is scenically as grand as before. The size of our group is gradually dwindling, a clear sign of the differing standards of fitness amongst the riders.

At the third feed station in Waldhausen (133km), some of the long course riders seem to be in a great hurry; in contrast to the relaxed short course riders, who now have only 40km left to cover. The long course riders must reach Geislingen by 12.30pm if they are not to go over the time limit. To the relief of the agitated racers, however, a one hour extension on the limit is announced.

After a swift descent to the main road for Geislingen, the turn-off point for 175 kilometres is passed. Perhaps it is worth mentioning that any black spots, which need to be negotiated with care, especially on the descents, are very clearly signposted by the organisers. The way ahead which forms a long loop is not very difficult, because of a gentle descent through a stretch of rolling countryside. Hardly have we settled down to this easy tempo when in Geislingen we are reminded not to forget the true nature of the event! On the outskirts of town there is a typical Alb climb, about four kilometres long with gradients of up to 10%, and we pass through shady beech forests on the way up to the

Organisational Information

Date – Late June

Distance – 255 and 175 kilometres

Total hill climbs – 4400 and 2800 metres

Highest climbs – Approximately 200 at 18% on leaving Reichenbach and about 200 metres at 16% after Stötten.
The event follows a hilly route with a further 15 climbs between 6% and 12%

Gearing – 42x26/28

Start place – 'Im Buchs' sports complex, Ottenbach. Take Ulm-West exit from the Munich–Stuttgart motorway, then follow signs for Eislingen, Süssen, Salach and Schwäbisch-Gmünd. The starting point is signposted from Geislingen

Accommodation – Hotels and campsite in Ottenbach. Free overnight accommodation is available in the sports hall and club room at the start area. There is also a low cost campsite with good facilities

Start time – Between 5am and 6am, for the 255km and between 6am and 7am for the 175 route

Entry fee – DM40 or DM30

Feed stations – There are about five of them

Participants – About 1700

Contact address – Annelore Nussbaumer, Ringstrasse 1, D-7335 Salach, Germany

Further information – About 10km of the route are on roads closed to normal traffic. From 1992 two additional routes of 300km with 4800 metres of hill climb and 205km with 3200 metres of hill climb will be offered as options

summit of the Alb in the direction of Bad Überkingen. Beyond that point the route heads towards Bad Ditzenbach (165km) through a varied, gently rolling landscape, through pasture land and small areas of deciduous forest.

Before we reach the feed station in Boll (185km), with its historic chuch, one of the oldest ecclesiastical buildings in the Stauferland region, we must attack another climb with gradients of up to 12% – the real 'killer stretch' is still to come. It lurks beyond Reichenbach, where the gradient increases to 18% over a 200 metre section. In lowest gear – which is still too high – we call upon our last reserves of strength to overcome this obstacle with our best effort.

Anyone who imagines that he now has the main climb behind him, will find to his surprise that after a short descent a further climb looms ahead. Only then does the road roll back to Geislingen (217km), which occupies almost the whole valley basin at the foot of the Steige range, and is surrounded by wooded or rocky hillsides. At the 225 kilometre point we reach the junction for the

shorter route and with it the last lengthy climb of about 3.5km at 10%. Anyone who happens at this point to pass short-route riders, who are just as battle weary but admirably unbowed, will experience an unexpected boost to his motivation. At 230 kilometres just before the last short climb there is a small feed station reserved exclusively for riders on the longer course.

Over the last 25 kilometres, which are certainly not flat, but do not present any severe climbs, it is remarkable that many of our fellow cyclists find time and energy for a chat. Up on a high plateau, cycling past a broadcasting tower and modern windmills, we can see the landmark of the region to the west – the Hohenstaufen. As the road rolls down to the bustling finish area we realise it is our last descent (250km). Race cards are collected and we immediately receive a computer printed certificate showing our time for the day's ride, and we proudly accept our exclusive sweatshirt. Then, according to our mood and enthusiasm we can quench our thirst in the beer tent to the accompaniment of a genuine German band.

These days it's hardly possible to organise an event without the aid of computers

66

Dolomite Marathon — 10

Italy

The Langkofel Range forms a beautiful backdrop on the climb to the Pordoi

If there were a prize for the touring event with the most beautiful scenery, it would have to go to the Dolomite Marathon. The setting provided by the Dolomites can only be described as magnificent. Of the countless cliffs, jagged peaks and rock-faces which tower up from the green mountain pastures only a few can be mentioned, such as the infamous Cinque Torri, the glacier fields of the Marmolada, the imposing Langkofel and the mighty Sella. The route guarantees that these scenic highlights can be fully savoured, and hardly one well-known mountain range is omitted. Considering the magnetic attraction which the Dolomites holds for cyclists, one is almost tempted to write 'only' in front

of the number of participants, which is around 1300. This tour may be beautiful, but its beauty is certainly matched by its degree of difficulty. Its total hill climb figure of 5000 metres is a magical one, especially if you have to climb them all on a bike, under your own steam, and in a single day.

Specialist mountain climbers are therefore advantaged, and they gather in plenty in Pedraces (0.0km), a small tourist village in the Gader valley. For the moment, the beauty of the Dolomites can only be guessed at, for here in this narrow section of valley between steep forest and pasture slopes, none of it can yet be seen.

Many participants may envy the small

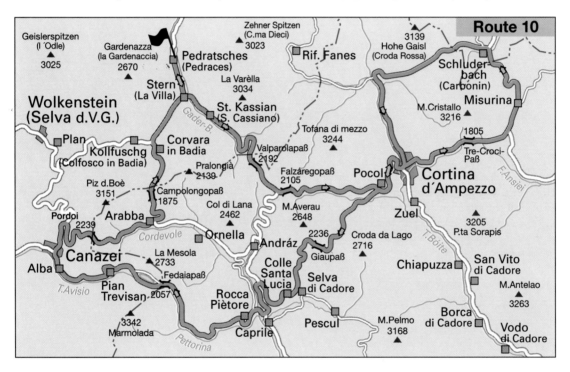

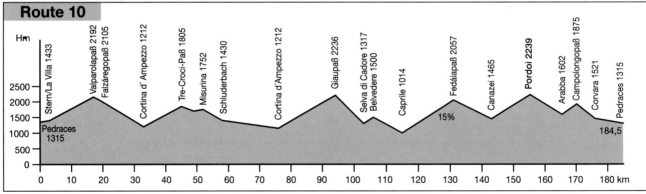

group of veterans and women riders, who set out at six o' clock at first light. On the stroke of seven the main field moves off and on a gently rising slope, arrives in La Villa/Stern (3km) almost intact, only to meet a bottleneck, for the road turns off sharply in the centre of the village for the first climb of the day, the Valparola Pass.

There is a short descent, on which it is advisable to engage your lowest gear ready for when the road climbs out of the village at 10%, easing off as the highest houses are reached. Even the short climb on the outskirts of St Cassiano (6.5km) does not lead into the start of the main climb itself. Continuing up to the Armentorola hotel complex (10km) we are again cycling almost on the level. The broad dry river bed of the Gader (11km) is crossed, beautiful larch and pine forests envelop us, and the 10% gradient is maintained up to the summit (16.5km). Up there a wasteland of scattered rocks awaits us, the rocky debris is the result of an avalanche on the Kleines Lagazuoi, followed by an almost straight line descent to the Falzarego Pass (19km). The route continues over its eastern slopes with downhill gradients of 11% and 21 hairpin bends. On the left the yellow and black scree of the Tofanen range dominates the view, whilst across to the right hand side of the valley is the Cinque Torri, and ahead is the Ampezzo range. The view over the roofs of Cortina d' Ampezzo, is the most beautiful of all; it opens out quite suddenly revealing a spectaculer green valley as we emerge from a short tunnel through the rocks

This elegant Olympic village (35km), venue for the winter games of the 1956 Olympics, is soon left behind and as we climb to the Tre Croci pass we begin the circuit of the Cristallo range. This is one of the smallest, yet most wild and beautiful ranges in the Dolomites. Even the initial climb is challenging. Admittedly the gradient remains at around 8% at the start, but then it increases to 11%, and as the route continues, it is always between 9% and 11%. As the summit approaches (44.5km) the view of the mountains behind us becomes ever more impressive: in the southwest are the Tofanen range, the Col di Lana, in the distance the snow fields of the Marmolada, the jagged peaks of

Organisational Information

Date – Early July

Distance – 184.5 and 151.5km

Total hill climbs – 5000 and 3770 metres

Highest climb – Approximately 1.5km at 15% on the Fedaia Pass

Gearing – 42x26/28

Start place – Pedraces in the Gader Valley

Accommodation – Hotels in and around Pedraces

Start time – Massed start at 7am. Women riders and competitors over 50 years of age start at 6am

Entry fee – 35000 lire

Feed stations – There are about 5 stations en route

Participants – About 1300

Contact address – SC Alta Badia, I-39036 Pedraces, 3(BZ) Italy

Further information – In order to encourage riders to take part in the event regularly the organisers intend to change the route every two or three years

the Croda da Lago and the huge tor of the Monte Pelmo. At this point a feed station would be more than welcome, but before that there is a descent with a 12% gradient down to the Misurina/Auronzo crossroads (48.5km) followed by a short but severe climb which brings us to Misurina (51.5km) in its wide grassy valley. The imposing twin-peaked summit in front of us is the Drei Zinnen, whose world famous north face lies hidden

On the middle section of the climb to the Pordoi these riders have already covered about 150km

The eastern side of the Falzerego Pass, shortly before the road branches off to the Giau Pass

from us, yet to be encountered as the tour progresses.

A road leads off in that direction, 7.5 kilometres long with a 16% gradient, which the organisers, thankfully, have not included on our route. Instead the road descends to Schluderbach (57.5km) with some 11% gradients. The road leading to Cortina d' Ampezzo (76km) is a good 18 kilometres long and really easy, so we can take time to admire the impressive view of the north face of the Monte Cristallo. In Cortina d' Ampezzo (76km) we have completed the loop, and now we attack the climb to the Falzarego Pass, already familiar to us having ridden the descent. We ride only as far as Pocol (81.5km) where the road branches off to the Giau Pass.

In fact before the next ascent begins,

there is a two kilometre descent to put behind us. Fortunately we do not lose too much altitude and we quickly replace it as we climb the 12% gradient up the road. After this, the average gradient is 10% and the road seldom dips below this figure. It is noon by the time we reach the summit (92.5km). Here we are provided with food and our race cards are stamped. It seems as if we could reach out and touch the Marmolada, but on the descent it moves back into the horizon. The well-surfaced road continues down the south-west slopes, and we contend with many curves, hairpins and steep downhill gradients. We have to brake sharply as we join the 251 main road (102.5km).

At Pian, whose church makes a photogenic subject with the Monte Pelmo towering behind it, and at the Colle St Lucia we again come across settlements, but then the road rises again gently to the viewing point signposted 'Belvedere' (106km). This location is aptly named, for the view of the almost 2000-metre high north west face of the Civetta – one of the mightiest of all alpine faces – is perhaps the most impressive to be seen in the Dolomites, which are certainly not lacking in beauty.

The road descends again as far as Caprile (113.5km) where we cross the River Cordevole, and in Saviner di Laste (115km) there is an opportunity to follow the shorter course. The shorter distance only amounts to a saving of 30 kilometres, but there is a saving in altitude of more than 1200 metres. The first part of the longer course involves a 15km climb to the Fedaia Pass, where the gradient rarely reaches 10% on the lower sections, but increases to 15% on the last 1.5 kilometres on the stretch up to the summit (130.5km). After a 14-kilometre descent to Canazai (144.5km) we face the 12.5-kilometre climb to the Pordoi – the highest point of the tour. Here the average gradient of 8% is exceeded only a few times on the lower slopes of the climb.

In Arabba (166.5km) the riders meet up again at the checkpoint and attack the last obstacle, the Campolongo Pass. The 8-10% gradients wouldn't be so bad if our legs were not already feeling the effects of so many other climbs. Finally, we reach the descent which leads to the finish line and use up those last reserves of strength.

The wide east face of the Langkofel makes an impressive setting for the race and no doubt is one of the attractions for these riders

Arber   **11**
Marathon ▬▬▬
Germany

The route through the Bavarian Forest is quite moderate as shown here in Viechtach

There are more than 1000 touring events held annually in Germany but there are very few whose importance is anything more than regional. Untypically, the Arber Marathon, first staged in 1986, has quickly succeeded in establishing itself and its fame has spread far beyond the confines of its region. The fact that the Arber Marathon is a Europa Cup event no doubt contributes to its success, but the enthusiasm of the organisers is admirable and the results speak for themselves. The route runs through the Bavarian Forest, a range of hills in eastern Bavaria close to the Czechoslovakian border. It's also worth mentioning that the course covers countryside whose natural beauty and unspoilt nature makes it one of the most beautiful holiday spots in Germany. As if this were not sufficient, the race is favoured by Walter Röhl, several times world rally champion and now an enthusiastic amateur cyclist, as a regular competitor there can be no doubt that he has

A hair-raising descent from the Scheibensattel down to Bayerisch Eisenstein. In the background sits the **King of the Bavarian** *Forest the* **Grosse Arber**

An immaculate
riding style on the
descent makes it
possible to reach
a good 70kph

contributed to the popularity of the event in Germany. The hill climb total of 3300 metres is also a great attraction to anyone wishing to test his form and condition.

Despite the staggered start, most riders are on the starting line for the stroke of 6am and they are sent on their way in small groups at short intervals. The use of cycle paths is strictly observed, and it is only on the outskirts of town that the first attacks are launched. Those riding at a more leisurely pace will catch sight of the Valhalla (9km) on the wooded slopes to the left: a folly built in the form of a Greek temple, which was commissioned by King Ludwig I of Bavaria in 1830 and completed by his architect Leo Von Klenze in 1842. It took 12 years to build.

Passing the crossroads, the Danube Valley is soon left behind and in Unterlichtenwald the first climbs begin. The countryside skirting the Bavarian Forest is very welcoming, an open rolling landscape,

Organisational Information

Date – Late July

Distance – 250 and 125 kilometres

Total hill climbs – 3300 and 1100 metres

Highest climb – 15% for about 500 metres on the outskirts of Kötzting. 11% for about 1.5km on the outskirts of Klingelbach. Other hilly stretches are mostly below 8%.

Gearing – 42x26

Start place – Regensburg, at the Danube shopping centre car park

Accommodation – Hotels and campsite in Regensburg

Start time – Staggered start times between 6am and 7am

Entry fee – DM50 or DM25

Feed stations – There are 4 *en route*

Participants – 2,000

Contact address – Veloclub Ratisbona e v, Pflanzenmayerstr 8a, D-8400 Regensburg, Germany

completed the first section of climbs and the route is mainly downhill as far as Cham (50km). The first checkpoint and feed station is on the outskirts of town, so our route only bypasses this place which has been fought over through the centuries because of its strategic position on the old trading routes to Bohemia.

The road is flat as we ride along the broad Regen Valley to Chamerau (63km) where we leave the valley and take the country road to Kötzting, a short cut but one which involves an 8% gradient. As we leave Kötzting (74km) there is a sign indicating a 15% gradient; now is a good time to find the lowest gear again. Riders who find themselves in the midst of a bunch will, at this point, hear others shouting questions about the length of the climb, even before they have had time to change gear. The answers differ greatly and so allow no assessment of the situation, but according to my odometer the road levels off to a great extent after 500 metres, and continues rising gently to a small hilltop (77km). An equally steep descent follows this steep climb, and brings us to the 'Lamer Winkel', an elevated valley through which flows the white Regen River. The mountain ridges are considerably higher here; they tower ahead of us in the form of long dark forest barriers, divided by road in the early stages. This is the upper Bavarian Forest, where the mountains, rising to heights of more than 1400 metres, around Osser, Arber and Falkenstein form the border with Czechoslovakia.

In Lohberghütte (95km) the road climbs again, and although it may have been possible to complete the climbs so far in the protective slipstream of a group, this next climb sorts the sheep from the goats! The gradient remains steady and does not exceed 6% but it lasts for the next eight kilometres up to the Scheibensattel (103km). Anyone seeing the rider in front gradually, but relentlessly, disappearing into the distance will take little comfort from the fact that the approaching level section past the Hindenburg Kanzel (105km) to the Sporthotel Brennes (107km) will provide one of the finest views to be had of the King of the Bavarian Forest – the 1456 metre Mount Arber with its distinctive adornment of two silvery steel spheres, which form

whose hilltops and hollows are chequered with fields, pastures and woodland – edged by road. There is a gentle undulation to the road and a 6% gradient is rarely exceeded. Shortly before Gfäll (31km) we enter the Bavarian Forest Nature Park, there's no noticeable change to the landscape, the gradient increases to 10% for 500 metres. After Falkenstein (36km) the first sizeable town after the start, the road drops away steeply, so there is little time to catch sight of the ruined 'Castrum Valkenstain' fortress of an old robber knight.

In Völlig the road again climbs on a 6% gradient to the little church of St Quirin (41km), which stands on a grassy hilltop above panoramic views. At this point we have

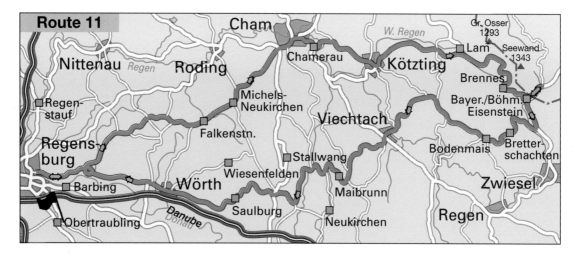

Route 11

the radar station. Sadly, this rider will be more concerned with trying to make contact again on the long descent to Bayerisch Eisenstein (113km).

The opening of the Iron Curtain in 1990 has made it possible to include a short trip across the border into Czechoslovakian territory to Böhmisch-Eisenstein. Back again on the E53, we have a few level kilometres ahead before we turn off abruptly near Regenhütte. There we reach the next checkpoint and feed station but we are also faced with the climb up the eastern slopes of the Grosser Arber. From the feed station the road rises at a gradient of 8% for the next 4.5km to the crossroads at the Aberseehaus (125.5km). Unfortunately, the lake and its charming setting are hidden from sight, and the course climbs for another 3.5km to Bretterschachten (133.5km), the highest point of the tour at 1120 metres.

After these exertions, the steep descents to Bodenmais (139.5km) and the mainly level or gentle downhill stections to Viechtach (164km) are very welcome. To the south of the Ostmark road, which is crossed at this point, more hilly countryside and climbs of up to 7% lie ahead. In Kolmberg (175km) it is advisable to make use of a small feed station, for now the last serious obstacle awaits us: 'the Ramp' a 1.5km climb with an 11% gradient. With that crossed, the worst is behind us; the road leads, with just a few short climbs, as far as Saulberg (221km). After this the main road ahead is as flat as a board. In Wiesent we welcome the first sighting of a signpost for Regensburg, our destination. The Danube comes into view (234km), and the Valhalla now glows in a different light. But it is a real disappointment to find the tables and benches for the tour finishers' supper already occupied by the short course riders!

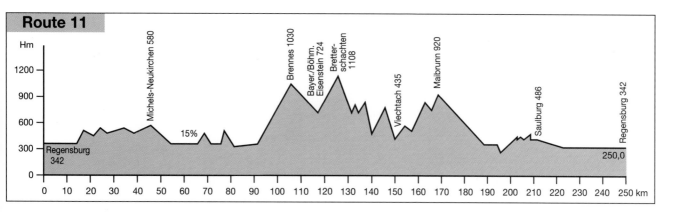

Öztal **12**
Marathon
Austria

The Öztal Marathon makes the superlative claim that it is the 'most difficult in the world'. It is not easy to test such boasts simply on the grounds of objective data such as the length of the course and total hillclimb figure. The latter figure does, however, make this tour unique! But just how one does validate such a claim is a conundrum – for instance against the Trondheim–Oslo's incredible 540 km, a distance one might more usually cover by plane; or the 265km from Paris to Roubaix where the cobblestone sections make great demands on the rider's physical condition and equipment not to mention the mental challenge that it presents. The Brevet des Randonneur des Alpes also stands comparison, boasting only a little less altitude with its 5400 metres of hill climb, but a considerably longer course at 300km.

Whether it is the most difficult or not, The Ötztal Marathon is without doubt an extreme challenge, which only the fittest of riders should attempt.

Dawn breaks over Innsbruck as the participants take up their start positions in separate lanes outside the Olympic ice rink (0.0km). The silhouette of the Karwendel Range, limestone cliffs to the north, is barely distinguishable in the chill morning air; the start is exactly on time at 6.15am and with our legs still stiff from the cold we make our way through the town. The early tempo is already brisk, for some of the riders are trying to better the fastest time and win the prize offered for the fastest finisher. This year the prize is a weeks skiing holiday for two. Most of the participants will not be giving this any thought as they turn into the Sellrain Valley, which is still in darkness at this time of day.

So far the course has been level, and alongside the river Melach the road rises only slightly. The situation changes in Gries am Selrain (19.5km) where, on leaving the village, the gradient increases to 16% for 500 metres. When the last riders have struggled up this section the leaders are already approaching the long scree slopes below the summit of the pass, having already climbed the 10% gradients interspersed with long fairly level sections. The sunshine, which has reached the summit before the cyclists, bathes the ancient, hilly landscape around

The tight hairpin bends on the descent from the Timmelsjoch demand precise riding skills

the winter sports resort of Kühtai in a warm light. The first feed station at the Kühtaisattel (32km) is a welcome sight. The road then drops into the Ötz Valley on a 17 kilometre descent over exceptionally good roads. In addition to the curves and hairpin bends, some cattle grids and steepening descent of 16% demand constant concentration and caution.

In Ötz there is one of the longest and highest valleys in the Alpine region separating the Öztal Alps in the west from the Stubai Alps in the east and after 49km into the race the long climb up the valley begins. Most of this stretch involves a gentle climb or in some places is even level, and it is only Habichen (51km), Sölden (77.5km) and Zwieselstein (82.5km) that we are faced with steeper climbs. The longest and most difficult of these comes after Zwieselstein, where the road climbs by 12% for three kilometres before descending again gently to Untergurgl (89.5km). Even there we have not finished for the road again climbs to Timmelsjoch.

Many riders, attacking the four numbered hairpins, clearly signposted as having altitudes of 12% on the way up to the Mautstelle (94km), might wish to go back to the time when the route was ridden in the opposite direction, and they could have freewheeled all the way downhill without difficulty. The road does descend from the Maustelle, however, for a good two kilometres at 10% and leads down to the barren limestone, mountainous region of the Tummel Valley. But a downward route is not really welcome at this point as it costs us valuable altitude gained on the way to the summit. Laboriously, we struggle to pull it back over the next five kilometres by way of six hairpin bends at an even gradient.

At the summit (104km), the view in fine weather extends beyond the Sarntal Alps, beyond Schlern and Langkofel as far as the Marmolada. For the most part, we concentrate on our more immediate surroundings, and in particular the inviting sight of the third feed station. Half of the tour is behind us, but the other half lies ahead and motivates us to cut short our stop. Quickly we fill our drinking bottles, thrust another piece of cake in our mouths, and one or two bananas into our jersey pockets. The 27 kilometre

Organisational Information

Date – Early September

Distance – 229 kilometres

Total hill climbs – 5500 metres

Highest climb – 16% for about 500 metres on the Kühtaisattel

Gearing – 42x26

Start place – Innsbruck, Olympic Ice rink

Accommodation – Hotels and campsites in Innsbruck

Start time – Massed start at 6.15am

Entry fee – 350 Austrian schillings

Feed stations – There are five

Participants – About 1600

Contact address – Radclub 88, Dr Stumpfstrasse 45a, A-6020 Innsbruck, Austria

Further information – In 1991 the tour direction was changed for the first time since 1985, and the climb of the Kühtaisattel came in the first section of the route. The start was also changed from Mutters to Innsbruck. Since we are concerned with the most up to date information, the account in this chapter follows this route. The organisers reserve the right, however, to run the tour in the opposite direction at a future date. For safety reasons, support vehicles are banned on the climb of the Kühtaisattel between Kematen and Ötz, and on the descent from the Brenner on the old Roman road between Matrei and Innsbruck

The last metres to the summit of the Jaufen Pass. The Brenner Pass still lies ahead but this rider already has the worst behind him

descent to St Leonhard in the Passeier Valley is before us; the road surface is poor. There is no comparison with the descent from the Kühtaisattel, unlit tunnels on the upper sections, tight hairpin bends, 13% gradients and heavy traffic make the experience less than pleasurable.

The route branches off at a sharp hairpin in St Leonhard (131km) and with virtually no level stretch after the descent, we begin the 21km climb to the Jaufen Pass. This in itself is difficult enough, but with the metres we have climbed so far, our legs find it a struggle. The gradient is mostly between 8% and 10%, only a few easier sections assist our progress, and the 800 metre level stretch, in the dimly lit tunnel, on the outskirts of Waldon, is a welcome exception. Feed station number four at the Gasthof Innerwalden (144.5km) provides a break during the descent, and we are ten kilometres away from the summit. On the 10% gradient we must not relax our effort, for when we make it to the summit (154km), we will have the worst behind us. Admittedly there is still the Brenner Pass ahead, but this is by far the easiest of the four climbs.

The descent to Sterzing is difficult, for the road surface is in such condition that can

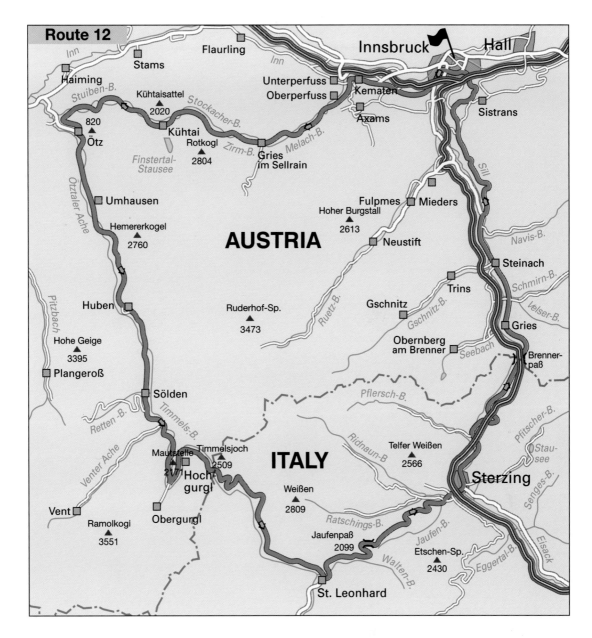

Route 12

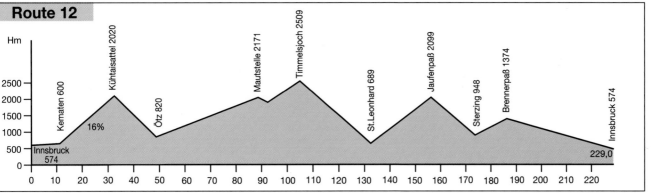

Route 12

only be described as catastrophic. Complete concentration is required as far as Gasteig (169.5km), and then we need to pedal again on the level stretch to Sterzing (172.5km). Leaving Sterzing the road rises gently, and on the way to Gossensass (178.5km) there are three dimly lit tunnels to negotiate before the route becomes difficult again. For about 600 metres the gradient increases to 12% and then drops to 6% becoming less as we go higher, and here we can catch our breath. From Brennerbad (186km) the road is almost level as we approach the summit.

It is not advisable to ignore the last feed station in Wolf Bei Stretch (195km) on the descent, as this refreshment may be much needed. In Matrei (204km) the route turns off to the old Roman road, which links the little parishes on the eastern side of the Wipp Valley between Innsbruck and Matrei. Even though this diversion was mentioned in the tour programme, a route marshal would have been helpful, as the notice at the junction in Matrei was missed by more than one rider.

As the locals say, 'all roads lead to Innsbruck' and it's true. The old Roman road has few surprises for us as we soon realise on the 10% climb up to Pons, which lasts for nearly 300 metres. For quite a long way the road clings to the slopes of the valley without losing much height, and between Pons (205.5km) and Ellbögen (212.5km) we repeatedly encounter short but easy climbs. After Patsch (214.5km) there is a checkpoint then the road drops down to the Inn valley, where the sprawl of Innsbruck's housing (227km) lies framed by the northern chain of the Karwendel Range. In the stadium (229km) the applause of the spectators seems to embarrass many of the finishers, but after such a hard-won achievement there is no reason why it should.

View from the old Roman road between Pons and Ellbögen after a good 210 kilometres

Other cycling events

*I*n Germany alone there are more than 1000 touring events organised annually. Most other European countries organise a similar number. It is therefore understandable that our selection is limited to a just a few of them. The tours described in the following pages are similar to cycle racing's classics, which enjoy a long tradition, and have become well known. In many cases they are considered to be the biggest or most scenic event organised in the locality.

Obviously, such a selection must always be subjective, and if one or another of the events which you consider especially worthy of inclusion yet has been omitted, I ask that you forgive me. You can obtain a list of all cycle touring events held in Germany if you send a stamped addressed envelope to:

Bund Deutscher Radfahrer
Otto-Fleck Schneise 4
6000 Frankfurt Main
Germany

From this same address you can also obtain a list of European cycling associations, and then you can request a list of all the touring events organised by that country.

A line of flags by the Gasthof Hochfirst greets the riders on the lower part of the descent from the Timmelsjoch

Stunning views are afforded by this recently built road above the village of Schröcken, on the climb to the Hochtannberg Pass

According to the organisers, the landscape of the Bregenz Forest provides the backdrop for 'Austria's greatest international touring event' – the Tour of Vorarlberg. This tourist region between Arlberg and Lake Constance has not been a forest in the true sense of the word for a long time. Sizeable, continuous wooded areas are only to be found in the ravines on northern facing slopes, and as protective woodland above the villages. Otherwise meadows, pastures and open alpine grassland, over gently rolling hills give this landscape its distinctive character. The challenging route of 170 kilometres with its hill climb figure of 1800 metres is not over-taxing and passes through the largest district of the Austrian province of Vorarlberg. Those riders who look forward to both the sporting element of the event and to enjoying the scenary *en route* are well catered for.

Hohenems (0.0km), the main starting point, lies on the edge of the Rhine Valley, where the Bregenz Forest comes to an end on steep bushy slopes with their scattered limestone crags. Keeping to the start line is not taken seriously here, and the first riders leave even before six in the morning, while still others take their time to complete a hearty breakfast underneath the main stand of the small football and athletics stadium of Herrenried.

The first kilometres in the Rhine Valley are flat. A cycle path can be used as far as Dornbirn (5km), where marshals are positioned at the larger crossroads, and then the first signposts for the Bregenzer Wald (Bregenz Forest) are encountered. After Schwarzach (13.5km) we leave the Rhine Valley and begin the 8% climb leading into the Bregenz Forest. This lasts for more than two kilometres through the narrow, thickly wooded river valley. The gradient eases by the time we reach Alberschwende (17.5km), where we ride out into the sunshine again. In the hilly landscape of forest and meadow land which appears before us, the imposing forest chalets with their splendid, stone-built lower storeys which are topped by moss covered beams and grey wooden shingle cladding, are extremely impressive. In the typical architectural style of the region, living quarters stables and haylofts are brought under one roof. There is a long downhill stretch to Egg (27.5km), which you would not think of as the biggest town and business centre in the Bregenz Forest. We come to a halt by the Gasthof Ochsen, and collect our first checkpoint stamp. There is a short 8% climb towards Andelsbuch (29.5km), and then we ride along the level road in the Bregenzer-Ache valley. The valley narrows into a gorge from time to time and then opening out wide again, twists its way through this mountainous landscape.

From their valley homes, people set out for church, some of the farming women are wearing their traditional costume: the 'Juppa', a skirt made of black glazed linen and boasting of more than 600 pleats. At Schoppernau (55km) we reach the end of the valley stretch and the sizeable groups of riders, formed during the long flat stage, break up at the checkpoint and feed station. The most difficult part of the tour lies ahead – the Hochtannberg Pass. As we leave the village we are faced with the first real climb, which passes through a 150 metre unlit tunnel and leads into a gorge-like section of the valley. Below the mountainous scree-slopes of the Hochkünzelspritze, the gradient decreases, only to steepen again at Hopfreben (62km), where the valley widens out again. We ride through a series of ice corridors and tunnels following the road that leads us to Schröcken (66km).

Once upon a time, this farthest corner of the Bregenz Valley, surrounded by nothing but forest and rocky crags, was the whole world for its inhabitants. These days things are obviously different and a well-made road ensures safe passage in summer and in winter. After fortifying ourselves at a small feed station on the outskirts of Schröcken we continue on our way. The new road is still a novelty, it has replaced the old road through Fuchswald, with its gradients of up to14%; the gradients now only reach 10%, and this continues over the next few kilometres to Schröcken-Nessleg (69km), then flattening out a little, it steps up to 11% for a short stretch. After the climb up to the summit the worst is behind us, although the summit (71.5km) is only the second highest point of this tour. It does give the best vantage point,

When the church in Rankweil comes into view after 150 kilometres, the finish line is not far away

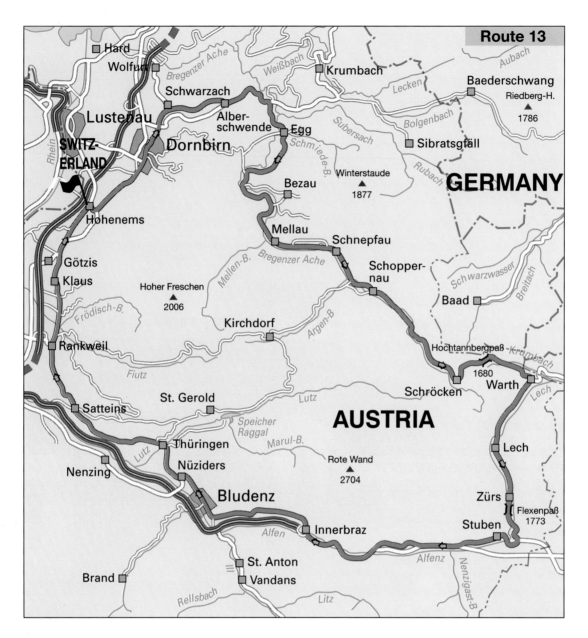

Route 13

Hard
Wolfurt
Schwarzach
Lusterau
Dornbirn
Alber-schwende
Egg
Krumbach
Baederschwang
Riedberg-H.
1786
Sibratsgfäll
SWITZ-ERLAND
Rhein
Bregenzer Ache
Weißbach
Lecken
Aubach
Bolgenbach
Subersach
Schmiede-B.
GERMANY
Hohenems
Bezau
Winterstaude
1877
Rubach
Götzis
Klaus
Hoher Freschen
2006
Mellau
Schnepfau
Schopper-nau
Baad
Schwarzwasser
Breitach
Kirchdorf
Argen-B.
Mellen-B.
Bregenzer Ache
Frödisch-B.
Rankweil
Fiutz
Lutz
Hochtannbergpaß
1680
Warth
Lech
Krumbach
St. Gerold
Satteins
AUSTRIA
Schröcken
Speicher
Raggal
Marul-B.
Thüringen
Nüziders
Rote Wand
2704
Lech
Nenzing
Lutz
Bludenz
Zürs
Flexenpaß
1773
Stuben
Innerbraz
Alfen
Alfenz
Nenzigast-B.
Brand
St. Anton
Vandans
Rellsbach
Litz
Litz

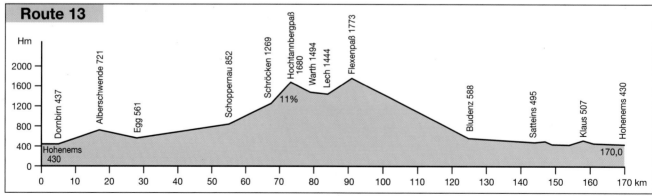

Route 13

Hm

Dornbirn 437
Alberschwende 721
Egg 561
Schoppernau 852
Schröcken 1269
Hochtannbergpaß 1680
Warth 1494
Lech 1444
Flexenpaß 1773
Bludenz 588
Satteins 495
Klaus 507
Hohenems 430

Hohenems 430

11%

170,0

Organisational Information

Date – – Mid August

Distance – 170 kilometres

Total hill climbs – 1800 metres

Highest climb – 11% on the Hochtannberg Pass

Gearing – 42x23/26

Start Place – Bludenz, Hohenems and Egg. Main start point is Hohenems at the Herrenried Sports Centre – well signposted from the Hohenems/Dipoldsau motorway exit

Accommodation – Hotels at all start places. Matresses are available in Hohenems, at the sports centre. There is also a free campsite with all facilities.

Start time – Staggered start times from 6am

Entry fee – 280 Austrian schillings

Feed stations – A food bag is provided at the start, additional food is available in Schoppernau, Schröcken, Flexen Pass, Hockrumbach and Bludenz.

Participants – About 1200

Contact address – ÖAMTC Radsportverein Hohenems, Achtrasse 20, A-6845 Hohenems, Austria

so its worth resting awhile at the feed station to enjoy the view over a flower-decked plateau. Here, a small tarn shines dark blue from out of the moorland, and above this, partly hidden from view by a small hill, rise the mighty, snow-flecked walls of the Mohnenfluh. The shapely summit of the Biberkopf in the east, part of the Allgäuer Alps, is worth a look but take care, for the road to Warth (76km) has some hair-raising downhills of around 10%.Here the route branches off sharply to the right into the upper valley of the Lech.The road falls away slightly but noticeably, on the way to the sophisticated ski resort of the same name (82.5km). The climb to the Flexen Pass, the highest point on the tour, is quite easy. At the start, a short climb of almost 7% through a small ravine leads into a tunnel about 200 metres long, followed by what seems like a never-ending ice corridor, where the gradient eases slightly. In Zürs (89km) we emerge into the open air again and the gradient seems to lessen as we approach the summit (90.5km). Another small feed station, then we freewheel over the southern side of the Flexen Pass, down to the junction with the Arlberg Pass road (94km). A marshal is stationed at the entrance to the Arlberg Pass road, a sensible measure, as the traffic on this important link road between Vorarlberg and Tirol is considerable. The road continues its descent, and beyond Langen (99km) we are able to leave this busy road turning on to the old Arlberg road. We continue, mostly downhill, to Blundenz (124.5km), through the Kloster Valley, reaching Blundenz around noon.

There is a great deal of traffic on the narrow, twisting streets of Vorarlberg, the provincial capital, but signposts make it possible to find our way easily to the checkpoint (127km). We are back in the Rhine Valley, where heavily built up areas alternate with open, agricultural land along the river banks. The mountains, rising above the northern side of the valley, need no longer trouble us, for the rest of our route runs along the valley floor. The road, which should be mentioned for the sake of the record, runs level but for two exceptions: there is a one kilometre 6% climb after Satteins (144km), followed by the descent to Göfis (147.5km), and a rather shorter 6% climb in Klaus (156.5km). It is hardly worth mentioning that the road rises gently again for about 100 metres on the outskirts of town, but for the fact that it is easy to lose the slipstream of a fast group at that point. After that the road opens up, and you will probably not be too upset to see at the finish that your odometer shows a few kilometres less than the 170 quoted in the route description.

On the long level section in the Bregenzer Ache Valley, sizeable groups of riders quickly form

Tour of Karwendel 14

Austria

'*F*aster, higher, further' proclaims the slogan of modern-day sport, and since this also applies to cycling, the International Tour of Karwendel has been extended from 180 kilometres to 250 kilometres by adding an extra loop. The date of the event was also changed from the beginning of September to the beginning of July. Many may regret this, for with the old date, riders from Bavaria and the Tirol, who make up the main contingent of competitors, welcomed the opportunity to

Organisational Information

Date – Early July

Distance – 250, 180, 123, and 36 kilometres

Total hill climbs – 1100 and 800 metres. Otherwise no major climbs

Highest climb – 12% for about 7lkm on the Buchensattel

Gearing – 42x26

Start place – Innsbruck, Technical University; for the 123km tour the Civic hall, Scharnitz

Accommodation – Hotels in Innsbruck and Scharnitz, campsites in Innsbruck

Start time – Massed start at 6am for the 250km course; staggered start times for the 180km course between 7am and 9am; staggered start times between 7.30am and 10.30am for the 123km course; staggered start times between 9am and 2pm for the 36km course

Entry fee – Between 60 and 290 Austrian schillings according to route length

Participants – About 1000

Contact address – ÖAMTC-Tirol, Herr Werner, Andechsstrasse 81, A-6020 Innsbruck or Horst Conrads, Richard-Wagner-Strasse 18, D-8034 Germering, Austria

finish the season with a really long tour. However, such change does not affect the scenic beauty of the tour.

At six in the morning there are a good 350 riders, about a third of the total participants, setting out on the 250 kilometre route from the starting point near the technical university (0.0km), on the western side of Innsbruck. The rest have chosen route C, described as the Karwendel Extreme, which, at 180km is challenging enough. The staggered start prevents confusion and jostling at the start line, and most riders only need queue for a little while before their tour card is stamped. The time is printed on the card at the same time as it is stamped, and when the card is handed in at the finish line the total time taken to complete the course is easily and honestly calculated. With such hard evidence to hand you can compare your time with friends who started earlier or later than yourself. The tour card also remains a record of your performance for subsequent years.

Once you have started, take care not to follow the signs for the short route which changes over to the south side of the Inn Valley before Kranebitten, and at 36 kilometres, is described as 'a family tour'.

The route keeps to the main road past the Gasthaus Kranebitten, where the road rises gently, only to drop away again immediately.

The tour of Karwendel is exceptionally well-signposted as this road sign for the next checkpoint shows

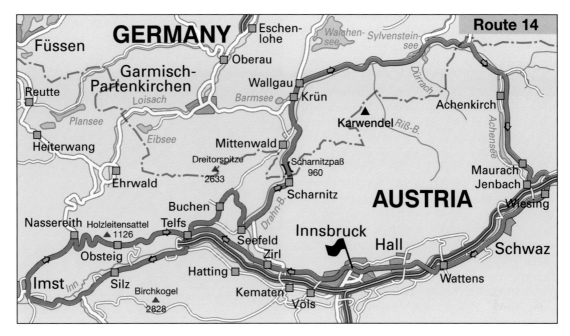

Dense bushland hides the view of the Martinswand rock-face, where climbing routes rated as 'extreme' lead up through its fissures. According to old legend, Emperor Maximilian I is said to have lost his way climbing here whilst hunting for chamois. He had to wait for three days before being miraculously rescued.

Continuing along the route, the Inn Valley opens out and provides a view of the peaks of the Mieminger Range, along the right-hand side of the valley. The road winds along the valley and stays almost level. We reach Telfs (24km) still feeling fresh. The riders on the 250km tour switch to the other side of the valley and continue to follow the course of the River Inn. After the checkpoint in Imst, the route leads us into the Gurgl Valley in the

direction of Nassereith. There we are faced with the climb to the Holzleitensattel, a 300-metre climb over five kilometres. The gradient on the well-surfaced road maintains an even 6% before it descends again, at first to 10% and then much more gently as it approaches Telfs. We have covered 70km more than the riders on the short course, who started out later. We meet up with them at the start of the climb to the Buchensattel. First, the road rolls into Sagl (96km) before rising to a gradient of 12% in a straight line – like a ramp – towards the summit.

In Bairbach (79km) we meet the first hairpin bend, and the Inn Valley lies far down below, as the road climbs as steeply as ever with its view of the rocky south face of the Hohe Munde. Riders are soon sorted

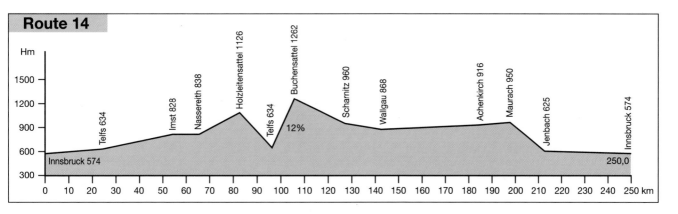

according to ability, like wheat from the chaf, long before this, but we all hope in vain for the gradient to ease. Then there are two hairpin bends, white Wetterstein chalk is thrown up from the edge of the road, another hairpin, and finally a checkpoint (103km) marks the end of this long climb. The welcome drinks come at just the right time, we have climbed almost seven kilometres, with the gradient hardly ever falling below 12%.

As we climb back into the saddle, we are certain that apart from the length of the course, no more serious difficulties lie ahead. We climb for another few metres, and at the Buchensattel we have reached the highest point of the tour. The road becomes narrower and more uneven as we speed down through dense deciduous forest into the green Leutasch Valley. This lengthy alpine valley, whose villages and surrounds provide the setting for several novels by local author Ludwig Ganghofer, and which has gained a reputation as a winter Eldorado for cross-country ski enthusiasts, provides us with an almost level road to follow.

People in Scharnitz (127km) may be puzzled by this renewed influx of cyclists. This little border town is the start point of the B tour, which spares its riders the most difficult section of the tour from Telfs to Buchen, but at 123 kilometres still leaves them no shortage of scenery, there is for instance, the Werdenfelser Region with Krun and Wallgau, two immaculate tourist villages which are easily accessible, and whose painted house facades almost succeed in distracting our gaze from the Wetterstein Range to the west. At the River Isar, which makes a sharp turn to the east in Wallgau (142km), we are entering the Isar loop.

A narrow toll-road runs between the Walchensee Mountains in the north and the Karwendel in the south. It has a few short climbs, which hardly reach 10%, and which are immediately cancelled out by corresponding descents. The bumpy and generally poor condition of the road does not allow for high speeds, and a checkpoint (152km) provides us with a short stop. In Vorderriss (156.5km) the road improves, and continues on the level to Fall (163.5km), with the exception of a few short climbs of up to 8% and some similar descents.

Lake Sylvenstein is crossed by way of the elegantly curved Fall George Bridge, and we ride along the left bank of the lake on the level. The road does not rise until we get to the end of the lakeside, as we approach the Kaiserwacht (174km). There is no longer anything to be seen of the old border post, which once guarded the border here, but we do meet the traffic pouring over the Aachen Pass in the direction of the Inn Valley. At the customs post in Aachenkirch (175km) we are once again riding in Tirolean territory. What interests us however, is that the lengthy climb of 10% at Gasthaus Marie (178km) is the last one of any importance.

Happiness is having a rescue and recovery service on hand

The limestone cliffs by the roadside on the climb from the Inn Valley to the Buchensattel, provide an almost alpine atmosphere

In Achenkirch (183km) there is another checkpoint. To our left rises the Rofan range, whilst the Achensee, one of the most beautiful lakes in the Tirol, comes into view ahead of us. It is also the biggest and so our lakeside ride seems to take forever, ending at Maurach (197km). Bumpy cobblestones on the Kanzel hairpin (202km) give us a thorough shaking. Meanwhile, far down below lies the Inn Valley, our route takes us down the long 8% descent to bring us painlessly into the bottom of the valley.

We ride under the motorway, across the River Inn, and anyone wishing to remove his windcheater has an immediate opportunity to do so at the last checkpoint just before Jenbach (212km). There are still almost 40 kilometres to go, but this stretch is not only level but also very quiet, as the motorway attracts most of the traffic.

By noon the first riders on the 180km route have reached Innsbruck, and those on the 250-kilometre tour are expected an hour later. There is amazingly little traffic, even through the centre of town, and at last the finish tape is in sight, a short final sprint and a stamp on the tour card. This entitles us to a handsome, engraved glass tankard, and a mention in the results list, which is published in the *Tirol Daily News*.

Senior Riders' World cup, St Johann
15
Austria

The outcome of this event is often decided on the climb to the Hubershoe, where most of the spectators gather

*I*t must be made clear from the start that the Senior Riders' World Cup is not a touring event but a race. There are nevertheless several reasons for including this event in these pages; the most important one being that any experienced cyclist who is 19 years old or more, can take part. The organisers require proof of age and some evidence of previous cycling experience, in addition to a cycle sports licence – obtained through membership of a club entitled to issue such documents. A further reason for including this event is that it is unique and its reputation is rapidly growing in stature so that it easily bears comparison with most other organised events. And maybe the best reason is that any cycling enthusiast would find it thoroughly worthwhile to participate at least once.

Before you do jump in, there are a couple of points that you need to be aware of and to be forewarned is to be forearmed. They do not concern the details of the event in terms of its organisation, execution and

financial commitment – all of which are thoroughly professional. The race itself harbours several potential problems, such as infighting, tough tactics, ruthless attacks, and drive to the point of exhaustion, all of which are diplayed by those who finish amongst the leaders. No professional race could be harder fought. Quite the opposite, in fact it is more likely that the professionals would ride it in a less dangerous and more relaxed fashion. Many a would-be racer tries to compensate for a lack of ability and experience by setting a hectic pace and showing excessive zeal. Falls occur quite frequently, and dangerous situations are the order of the day. The reader should not overestimate these impressions, which are admittedly subjective, and certainly not every rider will have felt the same way, or have experience of this sort of behaviour. It is certain, however, that a touring event is much less stressful, and consequently, the experience of success or failure is not so great.

The main field crosses the line in St Johann, where the leading riders have already finished

According to age group, competitors have to complete between one and three laps, which is 41 to 120 kilometres, and average speeds of up to 43km/hr are reached. Good racers and strong sprinters are favoured by the contours of the route, as the altitude difference is only 150 metres per lap. The climbs are nevertheless significant, and anyone falling behind here has hardly any chance of rejoining the main group because the average speeds are fast.

Between 40 and 90 riders, according to their age group, set off from the Wieshofermühle (0.0km), a short distance from the centre of St Johann. Very soon we reach the outskirts of town (0.5km), there is a short section on the 312 trunk road, and then we follow a side-road towards Kossen and Schwendt (1.5km). In the foreground, the Niederkaiser, a long, steep mountain ridge almost 1300 metres high, hides our view of the Wilder Kaiser. We have covered 25 kilometres when we reach the farms at Bärnstetten, and then the first, often decisive, climb to the Huberhöhe begins. This ascent is 2.3 kilometres long, rising in three stages, each interrupted by short almost level sections. At the start of the climb the large chainwheel can be used on the easy gradient, but this then increases to 8%, and the smaller chainwheel is necessary, soon followed by a larger gear sprocket, for on the last 200 to 300 metres the gradient increases to 10%. On a training run, such a climb would certainly pose no great problems, but when riding at race tempo, whilst gasping for breath and with legs feeling heavier by the second, the

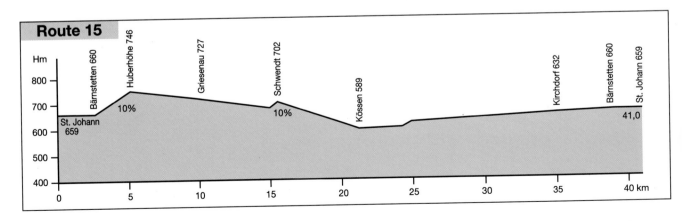

long climb seems vicious in the extreme.

Most spectators gather at the summit to cheer the riders on and lend them moral support. Perhaps the most help comes from the fact that road descends at this point – 5% down to Griesenau. On the left there would be a fine view of the rocky pyramids of the Wilder Kaiser, and we would have a glimpse of the Mauckspitze, Ackerlspitze and Lärchenspitze if our whole concentration were not directed to the road and the rear wheels of our rivals. Concentration is really needed here, for the road is in poor condition as a result of numerous repairs, and at the speeds reached on this section, our bikes need to be kept firmly under control.

The road levels off again at the Gasthof Mitterjager (6km) before it descends again (8.5km) quite gently and leads to Griesenau (9.5km). Slipstreaming is necessary for the next five kilometres, as the road is completely flat along the valley basin. Those familiar with the course start to use race tactics here, for the second climb leading up to Schwendt, is imminent and it too will leave its mark upon the field in the form of long gaps reaching back to the stragglers. This climb lasts for one kilometre, starting easily, then steepening to 8% by way of two hairpin bends, increasing again to 10% on the last 100 to 200 metres, as far as the Schwendt boundary sign (16km). Even here we cannot relax our efforts during the next 500 metres through the village, since the road continues to rise significantly, though not too steeply.

On the outskirts of the village (16.5km), we reach the first really long descent to Kössen (19.5km), and those who have fallen back on the climbs should try to regain their position now on these three kilometres of wide, well-surfaced road with its 10% gradient. There will be little opportunity for this at any other stage of the route. Before the actual town centre of Kössen, the road turns off sharply to the right onto the 172 trunk road. We cross the Grossache (21km) and a little later the road turns for home as we enter the Kössen Valley. There is however a small obstacle here, in the form of a 300 metre climb at 7%. Riders who have kept up with the lead group will have no difficulty in maintaining their position as the climb is too short to encourage attacks. There is a short

Organisational Information

Date – The event is held over seven days in mid August

Distance – One lap is 41km long. According to age group, one to three laps are covered

Total hill climbs – About 150 metres per lap

Highest climb – 10% on short sections during the climb to the Huberhöhe, and before Schwendt

Gearing – 42x21/23

Start place – St Johann, by the Wieshofermühle

Accommodation – Hotels and campsite in St Johann

Start time – Between 1pm and 1.40pm according to age group

Entry fee – 300 Austrian schillings

Participants – About 2000 competitors from 30 countries divided into 28 classes

Contact address – Senior Riders' World Cup, A-6380 St Johann in Tirol, Postfach 77, Austria

Further information – An insurance certificate is not required. Every competitor takes part at his own risk, and is liable for any accidents caused by himself, and for any consequences. Private third party insurance is therefore in the riders own interest. A crash helmet is compulsory. The races for riders without a licence are held on the first four days of the week long event. On the other days, races for riders with a valid FIAC-UCI licence are held. The final event is an amateur road race covering five laps

descent into the Grossache Valley (23.5km), and then there is only a level course between ourselves and the finish line.

Despite this, or perhaps for that very reason, single riders or small groups try repeatedly to shake off slipstreaming pursuers, and even try to force a small decisive break. This is a difficult undertaking, as the road is not only completely straight and level, but also very well surfaced. Shortly before we reach the 312 road, we turn off to the right (32.5km) onto a side-road running parallel to the main road. This continues on the level, but not so wide as before, and the road surface is rather poor in parts. The road twists along past the church in Kirchdorf, there are a few bends to be taken leaning into the curve, and then we roll onto Bärnstatten (39km), once again along a straight road.

According to the number of laps to be ridden, the climb to the Huberhöhe starts again, or alternatively, riders follow the approach section in the direction of the finish line. A sign indicates the last 2000 metres. Our turning onto the main road is made extremely safe, just like the rest of the race, by the presence of police and race marshals. Then we see the boundary sign for St Johann (41km), and all that's left is to ride the finishing straight. The official results are not released until a few hours after the last race at about 7pm. At 8pm the presentation ceremony begins, with the winner's national anthem, and cups are presented to the first 20 riders in each class.

On the Wildhaus Pass there is no need to force the pace for there are no more climbs in the remaining 100 kilometres of the race

The climb to Schwendt lasts for about one kilometre over a gradient of 10% maximum, and, tactically, is a key to the outcome of the race

International Tour of
Säntis ▬▬▬▬▬▬
Switzerland

16

The Alpstein is a range of mountains in north-east Switzerland, or to be more exact, in the canton of Appenzell. It dominates the landscape, with its three clearly defined chain of hills, looking down on the Rhine Valley and the basin of Lake Constance. At 2501 metres, the Säntis is the highest mountain in the Alpstein Range, and so this impressive landmark has given its name to the tour. It is said that nowhere in Switzerland do nature's vibrant colours glow so strong and clear as here in the Alpstein District: from the lush green of the meadows, the blue of the sky, the white of the clouds to the rich ochre of the local houses. Anyone who has taken part in the Säntis tour will confirm this fact. The landscape is charming, with hilly meadows, little hollows, scattered groups of trees and far-flung farmhouses. It all stretches out before us like a gently undulating carpet, towards the rocky fortress of Säntis. It is an easily sighted landmark with its soaring telecommunications mast, but it never comes into immediate reach, allowing itself to be admired at a distance as if aware of its star-ring role.

From the main starting point in Uzwil (0.0km) where a local has to point out the rocky summit, which towers in the distance to the south-east. Here at seven o' clock the world is still at peace, as we collect our food bags at the ice rink, get our drinking bottles filled, and ride out past the office blocks of the Büler Company in the direction of Uzwil. The first climb is in the village itself, 6% for a distance of 500 metres. Then the gradient lessens, and as we leave the village, we find ourselves on largely traffic free side-roads.

It is quiet here on this Sunday morning, hardly a car disturbs us. We will soon be feeling hot from our efforts, despite the morning chill. The surrounding countryside, known as Toggenburg, is gently rolling or fairly hilly. The road has to follow its contours – climbs alternate with descents, with level stretches here and there. The climbs hardly ever exceed 6%, and they are not very long at just a few hundred metres. There are quite a few flat sections, which help the pace and so we soon reach St Peterzell (25km). For the riders on the shorter course of only 58km this is already the point to turn for home, but hardly anyone takes advantage of the oppor-

tunity, and almost everyone continues with the route. The first test awaits us: the road climbs for a good two kilometres, its gradient increasing to 10%, by way of some hairpin bends. Then it eases off as we approach the first checkpoint in Hemberg (28.5km). There is another easier climb and then we are faced with a long descent to Obertoggenburg, which ends just outside Neu St Johann (38.5km). In a small car park on the outskirts of town we are able to take off our jackets, for now we are about to start a longer climb.

The landscape around us can best be compared to that of a fairytale. A giant is once said to have lived in the Alpstein District, and he hit upon the idea of building

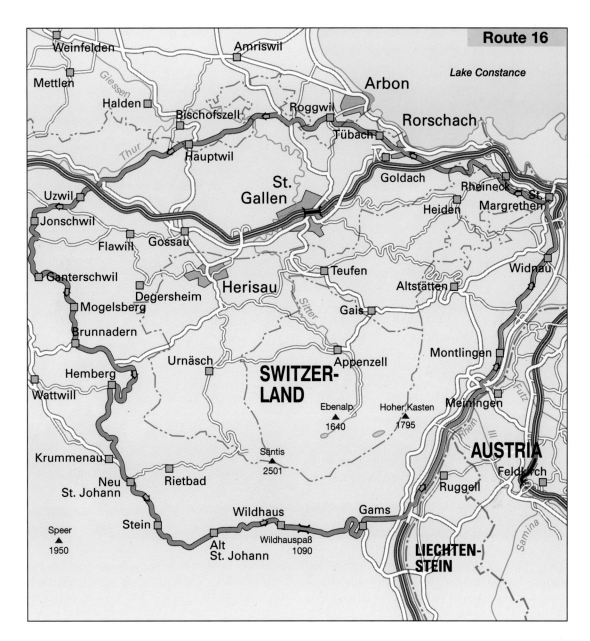

Weinfelden

Amriswil

Arbon

Lake Constance

Mettlen

Halden

Bischofszell

Roggwil

Rorschach

Tübach

Hauptwil

Thur

Goldach

Giessen

St.
Gallen

Rheineck

St.
Margrethen

Uzwil

Heiden

Jonschwil

Gossau

Flawil

Widnau

Ganterschwil

Teufen

Altstätten

Degersheim

Herisau

Sitter

Gais

Mogelsberg

Brunnadern

Montlingen

Urnäsch

Appenzell

**SWITZER-
LAND**

Meiningen

Hemberg

Ill

Futz

Wattwil

Ebenalp
▲
1640

Hoher Kasten
▲
1795

Rhein

AUSTRIA

Säntis
▲
2501

Feldkirch

Krummenau

Ruggell

Neu
St. Johann

Rietbad

Samina

Speer
▲
1950

Stein

Wildhaus

Gams

Alt
St. Johann

Wildhauspaß
1090

**LIECHTEN-
STEIN**

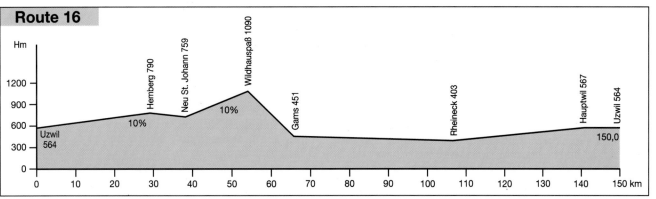

Route 16

Hm

1200

900

600

300

0

Uzwil
564

Hemberg 790

10%

Neu St. Johann 759

Wildhauspaß 1090

10%

Gams 451

Rheineck 403

Hauptwil 567

Uzwil 564

150,0

0   10   20   30   40   50   60   70   80   90   100   110   120   130   140   150 km

a town in the Obertoggenburg, which at that time was uninhabited. So he had houses built by dwarves who lived in the neighbouring town of Montafon, and he carried the houses home in a large sack. The sack was ripped open on the rocky crags, and the houses tumbled out like snowflakes down the hillsides, mountains and valleys where they have remained to this day. If you gaze at the scattered houses on the green mountain slopes, magnificently framed by the limestone mass of the Alpstein and Churfirsten, you might almost believe the story.

Back from fairyland, the reality of some gruelling climbs faces us. The road remains level as far as Nesslau (40.5km), climbs at 9% for 500 metres and then immediately eases again. Moderate climbs alternate with long flat

sections, and it is not until we reach Unterwasser (52km) that the gradient increases to 10% on the last kilometre before Wildhaus (53km). The road levels as we approach the centre of town (55km), and here at the highest point of the tour, we can marvel at the view of the rock face of the Wildhaus Schafberg, thrusting skywards behind the village church. Continuing a little further, we once again catch sight of the strangely formed Churfursten Range, which with its 13 adjoining peaks, plunges down to Lake Walen to the south. We throw ourselves into the long descent with its 15% gradient, and rush down to Gams (65km) in the Rhine Valley.

The second checkpoint is by the village school; we cross the Rhine valley and ride in the direction of Liechtenstein, where we turn

On the lower slopes of the Wildhaus Pass, such obstacles are to be expected

The descent from the Wildhaus Pass, the background shows the strangely formed Churfirsten Range

off onto the banks of the Rhine, just before we reach the principality (69.5km).

Ahead of us are 35 completely flat kilometres, initially on a road closed to normal traffic, following directly alongside the left bank of the Rhine, and then moving onto quiet side-roads through fertile arable land. Not until Au (100km) do we rejoin the main road, but we can still use a cycle path as far as Rheineck (107km). There is a great deal of traffic in this densely populated area at the eastern tip of Lake Constance, but it's a relief to be able to leave the main road again after Rheineck, to ride along country roads in the direction of Goldach. The route climbs at up to 9% however during the next kilometre, and then drops away again only to rise gently at Mount Rorschach.

The last part of the tour takes us into an area which can be described as tranquil. Extensive orchards alternate with fields of sunflowers and the occasional field of maize. The half-timbered houses are well suited to the landscape, and even the gentle undulations of the road do little to test our fitness. Gradually we are returning to the lower slopes of the Alpstein District. Open meadows replace the fields, and dark clumps of trees are scattered over rolling hillsides. This easy, undemanding tempo lasts until Hauptwil (140km) and then the road flattens out. The finish line in Uzwil appears all too soon, as a memento of the tour we can choose between a medal or, according to the number of competitors, a very appropriate and charming cow-bell.

Andermatt Alpine Trial 17

Switzerland

This rider ventures into barren, rocky regions, typical of the high peaks

*H*eld for the first time in 1977, the Andermatt Alpine Trial can already lay claim to an established history. Apart from the French Alpine Tourist Trial, this tour has long been recognised as the most difficult cycle touring event of all. Today both tours find themselves to some extent overshadowed by the Ötztal Marathon, which, despite not being able to claim the tradition of these events, can still offer a few extra metres of hill climb. Nevertheless, participation in the Alpine Trial, especially for fitter mountain specialists, is still worthwhile – not just for the potential achievement but also for the scenery. As more and more riders take up the mountain challenge the number of support vehicles increases accordingly, and with them the accompanying risks. For that reason, the organisers have decided to spread the event over two days for safety reasons. This is not a bad idea, since an extra day can be held in reserve in case of bad weather conditions. Since the organisers are involved in greater

The view across the glaciers of the the Bernese Oberland is only revealed just before the summit of the Nufenen Pass. On a clear day, like this, you can see the the peak of the Finsteraarhorn in the background

expense it remains to be seen whether this ruling will be maintained.

A mist hangs over the barracks in Andermatt (0.0km) but the weather forecast predicts a fine day. This cannot be taken for granted here at the beginning of September, when the approach of Autumn often brings rain, which can easily turn to snow on higher ground. Tour cards are stamped, there is some well-meaning advice, from a marshal who realises that I am without lights, to the effect that I should wait until the mist clears, but the urge for action is too great to allow time to slip by in this way. By the time Realp (5.5km) is in sight, the mist is disappearing, the Gotthard Range to the south is still in shade, but the mountains around Dammastock, high above us, are already bathed in sunlight. The road starts to climb as we reach the last houses of the small town, and we quickly gain height as we negotiate a series of hairpin bends and an 11% gradient.

At the Hotel Galenstock (10.5km) we can

Route 17

already make out the line of the road up to the summit.

We have long since taken off our jackets which were protecting us from the morning chill, and our ride up the unrelenting climb ensures that we stay warm. As we continue the gradient remains between 8% and 11%. At the top there are another two hairpins, and then we reach the Furka Hotel (17km) which sits at the summit of the Furka Pass.

It is best to wait until you have covered another few hundred metres before you pause to pull on your jacket for protection on the descent. It is at this point that you will be able to see the icy giants of the Bernese Alps to the far west, where above the twists and turns of the narrow road leading up to the Grimsel Pass, the peaks of the Fiescherhorn, Lauteraarhorn, and Eiger can be seen.

There is a long descent to Gletsch (30.5km) with gradients of up to 11%. We pass by the Rhône Glacier, which comes to

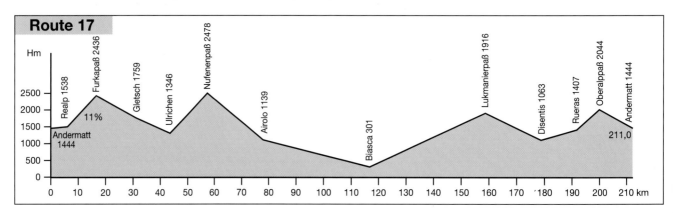

within a few metres of the road at the Hotel Belvedere. Less than 200 years ago this glacier completely filled the valley which lies below us. Arriving in the town we must take care to avoid the rails of the narrow gauge railway, which represents a considerable threat to our narrow tyres, not once but twice for on the outskirts of town we have to bump over these antiquated rails again. Crossing the shoulder of the valley, the road leads down to Oberwald with some steep descents.

We are now in Goms, as the highest part of the Rhine valley is called. Green meadows make the surroundings seem more welcoming, but the road, which is now level again, demands some effort. We leave the valley in Ulrichen (41.5km), an unspoilt village with typical dark wooden houses. We cross the Rhône near its source where it looks like an overgrown meadow stream, and then after 13 kilometres of hill climbing the Nufenen Pass lies ahead. There are several hairpins on the slopes of the southern side of the valley, as we struggle up the 10% gradient. After about three kilometres the climb eases off, the walls of the mountains close in on us, and 8% gradients alternate with flatter sections. An almost level one kilometre section marks the halfway point of the climb, and then we cross over to the left-hand side of the valley (47.5km). The gradient increases to 8% again, leading to a series of hairpin bends and then the road steepens to 10% as it takes us up to the summit (55km).

The view from the highest pass in the Swiss interior extends far into the Bernese Oberland, with the majestic peak of the Finsteraarhorn dominating the region. The feed station should not be missed; it will be the last for a long time. Putting on a jacket before the descent has become almost routine. Initially there are a few hairpin bends, then a 10% gradient, the road leads down through the Val Bedretto to Airolo (78.5km) in an almost straight line.

The riders on the short course can start their return journey over the Gotthard Pass, but most ride on through the Leventina Valley to Biasca. Here in the Sopraceneri, the northern part of Ticino, there is no hint of the Mediterranean plenty of its southern region, the Sottoceneri. This is a bare valley without charm, providing a route for railway and motorway, but at least it is on a slight

Organisational Information

Date – Early September

Distance – 211 and 104 kilometres

Total hill climbs – 4720 and 3100 metres

Highest climb – 11% on the Furka Pass

Gearing – 42x26

Start place – Barracks complex, Andermatt

Accommodation – Hotels and campsite in Andermatt

Start time – Staggered start times between 5.30am and 8.30am

Entry fee – 25 Swiss francs

Feed stations – There are five feed stations

Participants – About 1500

Contact address – Schweizer Rad und Motorfahrerbund, Postfach, CH-8023 Zurich or, E Fivaz, Lärchenstrasse 15, CH-9240 Uzwil, Switzerland

Further information – The event is held over the weekend during both days

downhill slope. In Biasca (116km), we branch off into the Bleni Valley, and soon reach a feed station where we can finally refill our water bottles.

The southern side of the Lukmanier Pass could not be described as difficult, but at 43 kilometres it is extremely long. In the early stages the road is level, and so the small chainwheel is not needed again until just after Malvaglia (124km), but then the gradient is mostly under 6% as far as Olivone (138.5km). Even then it does not increase dramatically. On the upper slopes beautiful forests line the route, and this alpine crossing is almost completely free of traffic. Eventually the Lukmanier Hospice appears at the top of the pass (159km). The summit does not provide any exceptional views, and only the extensive reservoir at the foot of the Piz Lai Blau offers some scenic variety.

The road follows the eastern bank of the reservoir, passing through a long corridor in the ice, and then starts to descend again. The concrete road surface, with its regular expansion gaps remind us of the descent from the Nufenen Pass, descending in a straight line at almost 10%. The Höllenschlucht Gorge on the lower slopes of the descent was once feared, but now has been made easier with the construction of some tunnels, which present new dangers. Even worse is the immediate 1.5km climb at 8% to Disentis (178.5km).

It is now well into the afternoon, the amount of traffic is increasing again, and we still have to tackle the climb to Oberalp Pass, involving high altitudes of a good 900 metres. For the next five kilometres, lengthy stretches of 10% climbs alternate with flat sections, before the road descends to Sedrun (187km). We are giving back hard-won altitude before the route climbs again at a moderate rate, as far as Rueras (191km). Then the Tavetsch, the uppermost part of the Rhine Valley, becomes narrower, and the gradient increases to 8% and 10%. It is neither Lake Oberalp nor the feed station which make reaching the summit such a pleasure but rather the fact that only a descent of 11 kilometres separates us from the finish line in Andermatt (211km)

Riding above the clouds on the Lukmanier Pass

These splendid half-timbered houses are becoming rare, even in the area around Lake Constance

*W*hen the first days of autumn arrive, the summer is almost gone, the days are shorter and the nights are cooler, the autumnal weather of wind and rain does its best to drive away the last vestige of summer, then is the time for the touring cyclist to round off his season with a rewarding and challenging tour.

The Tour of Lake Constance is long at 220 kilometres, but not too difficult, with a total hill climb figure of about 840 metres. It has become an almost traditional finale to the season, especially for riders from the countries adjoining the lake – Germany, Austria and Switzerland. As the title suggests the emphasis of the ride is on the touring aspect of the course; unlike a great many other events, the tour is aimed at those whose sights are not set exclusively upon their race time or a fast average speed. These goals would be difficult to achieve as a large part of the route runs along lakeside roads which feed densely populated areas, so the roads themselves are always busy. Cycle paths in the towns are often shared with pedestrians, and on country roads there is only a narrow strip for cyclists, separated from the main carriageway by a yellow line. This presents no problem if you are alone or with just a couple of others, but on a touring event such as this, space is at a premium especially when a faster group is hell bent on overtaking a slower one. Care and caution are required at all times, but this need not spoil your enjoyment of the tour.

From the six towns available as starting points, we have chosen the small town of Altenrhein (0.0km) for this chapter. It lies on the south-east side of the lake. As a result of the staggered start times, the car park by the small airport, used mainly by owners of private planes, fills up quite slowly, and so there is plenty of space to make preparations for the start. You can collect the stamp on your tour card at the same time as your food bag, whose contents are likely to end up in your jeresy pockets. When you start out, follow the clearly visible, orange route arrows.

With a length of 69 kilometres, and average width of 10 kilometres, a surface area of

The hilly hinterland of Lake Constance between Berg and Eriskirch on the German side of the lake

112

Organisational Information

Date – Mid September

Distance – 220 kilometres

Total hill climbs – 840 metres

Highest climb – 11% for almost 300 metres after the checkpoint at Meersburg Harbour

Gearing – 42x23

Start places – Altenrhein, Kreuzlingen, Stein am Rhein, Meersburg, Eriskirch near Friedrichshafen, Lindau

Accommodation – Hotels at all the starting places. Mass accommodation in Altenrhein, Kreutlingen and Stein am Rhein. Campsites in Altenrhein, Kreuzlingen, Stein am Rhein and Friedrichshafen

Start time – Staggered start times between 7am and 9am

Entry fee – 45 Swiss francs

Feed stations – A food bag and drinks are provided at the start. It is also possible to buy refreshments at any of the startpoints and checkpoints

Participants – The number of riders has been limited to 5000

Contact address – Radwanderfahrt Rund um den Bodensee, Radfahrer Verein, ch-9423 Altenrhein, Switzerland

Further information – Late applications are not accepted. Closing date for applications is one month before the event. The route is very well signposted, and supervised by traffic police and tour marshals, especially within the Swiss borders. Observation of the highway code is insisted upon by the police. Although no passport checks are made on riders at border crossing points as a rule, identification should be carried at all times

539 square kilometres and a depth of 252 metres, the lake has proportions of an inland sea, and our route for the most part follows its banks, but actually we do not catch sight of it very often.

We seem to pass directly from one town to the next. Their cultural heritage and art treasures remain unappreciated by the cyclists since they are too preoccupied with themselves and the traffic. In Arbon (11km), the first short climb competes for attention with the centre of the old part of town, and its castle – the Turmburg – an unusual sight after all the modern buildings we have seen so far. Gradually the surroundings become more rural, the villages no longer follow each other so closely, separated as they are by corn fields and orchards. Now and again the road rises slightly, but falls away just as quickly. It is sufficient to rise from the saddle to deal with these climbs without losing speed, and those riders who prefer to stay in the saddle will just need to change down one gear. In Altenau (30km), we are only a few metres above the lake, but we can look across open meadows and catch sight of the opposite bank. We soon reach the first checkpoint at the harbour in Kreuzlingen (38km) where heavily salted broth is dished out free of charge, it will soon replace any salt we have lost during the ride. Naturally any further food we require must be paid for; the food we received at the start is still not finished so the stop is easy on the purse.

Here in the north-west, the lake divides into Lake Überlingen and the Untersee, and we continue along the banks of the latter in the usual fashion. There are villages, houses, traffic lights and open stretches, which are mainly level, but occasionally include easy climbs and descents. Keeping in a group is difficult as there is not much room on the cycle paths, or roadside strips, riders must show discipline and ride single-file. In Berlingen (51km), with its beautiful half-timbered houses and lofty church tower, we find ourselves riding directly alongside the water for the first time. After Wagenhausen (68km) the route leaves the main road, and passes through farmland at the end of the lake. All support vehicles are diverted, but they shortly rejoin the field at the Rhine Bridge (70km).

The riders we see coming towards us at this

point have already reached the second check-point in Stein am Rhein (72km) where, contrary to the map in the official route description, the course does not run alongside the lake, but rather turns away a little, crossing the border at Ramsons customs point (78.5km). Although our surroundings appear to be quite hilly, the road here in the Swabian section remains very flat. The railway bridge as we come into Radolfzell (90km) is the first route climb.

Back on the banks of the lake, the road runs level as far as Allensbach (102km) and then crosses the Bodanrücken, as the promontory is called, which juts out like a peninsula far into the lake. The route constantly rises and falls gently, the climbs being mostly only 100 metres long, with a 6% gradient and gradually we climb higher through the thickly wooded, quiet countryside. After

about seven kilometres we reach the highest point (109km) and the road to Constance (119km) is then mainly downhill on an easy gradient.

At the harbour in Konstanz (120km) a lane is reserved for cyclists which leads to the crossing. There is a short wait until one of the boats of the *White Fleet* has tied up, and then solid ground is replaced by the ship's deck for a little over 10 minutes. The crossing can be exciting in rough weather, or if you are unable to find your tour card with its voucher for the crossing. The disembarcation in Meersberg takes place in a disciplined fashion: first the foot passengers, then the cars and finally the cyclists. The third checkpoint is at the harbour, and it is advisable to engage your lowest gear as you continue on your way.

After just a few hundred metres, the

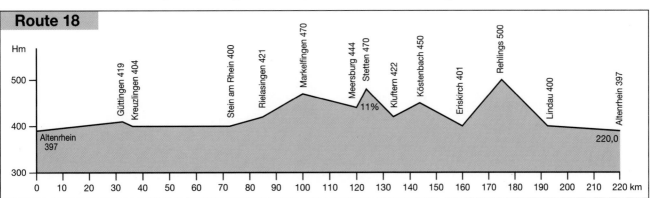

road turns off sharply to the right, a road signposted as a cul-de-sac leads uphill on a dark forest slope, and climbs for about 300 metres at a maximum 11%. More than a few riders are caught out by this unexpected climb, which leads to the upper part of Meersburg. They are unable to maintain enough momentum out of the bend to be able to change gear, and are forced to dismount or roll back a little to engage the gear. As we leave Meersburg on rural lanes alongside the main road, there are some more short climbs (maximum 9%) and then the steepest climb of the tour is behind us (126km). The road undulates gently as we head for Berg (145km), but it does not present any problems; there is very little traffic to bother us as we cycle through the maize, cereal and sunflower fields. We finally join the main road, which runs on the level to the fourth checkpoint in Eriskirch (160km)

After Nonnenhorn (170km) it becomes hilly once again. These climbs are not tough – hardly 7% and only a few hundred metres long – they are cancelled out immediately by a descent, but after the flatter earlier part of the route, they eventually begin to tell on our legs. This rolling countryside lasts until Schlachters (184km) and then we catch an early glimpse of the lake. The road heads downhill, just before Lindau at an even 13%. We reach the fifth checkpoint at the resort of Eichwald (191km) and then we ride along the lake to the customs point at Lindau (193km). Very soon we cross the Leitlach, and after passing through the Höbranz customs post, we are cycling on Austrian soil. Traffic can be a problem in Bregenz (197km) and when in the clearest of weather conditions, we look from here to the west, it is not always possible to see the ships sailing between Constance and Meersberg, because at this distance the curvature of the earth can hide them from view. It is a long time since the lake was last frozen over – in fact it last happened in 1963.

The finishing line is not far away: just another half an hour or so of level cycling to the customs post at Gaissen/Rheineck (213km) and then a few kilometres on the cycle path alongside the busy dual carriageway. The airport control tower comes into view, and very soon we are collecting our medals at the finish line (220km).

A short stop at the harbour in Constance as riders wait for the ferry to Meersburg

Nine Hills Apennine Trial 19

Italy

This peaceful, traffic free section away from the Adriatic coast more than compensates for the poor road surface

For professional cyclists spring is the time of one-day classics, held mainly in the cycling obsessed countries of Belgium, France and the Netherlands. There is the opportunity to ride hot on the heels of the professionals and in similar style, as mentioned in the earlier chapters of this book – in such races as Omloop Het Volk, Liège–Bastogne–Liège, or Paris–Roubaix. But for anyone who does not relish the prospect, especially in the often unreliable, rainy weather at this time of year, or the stormy winds on the plains and hills of Flanders, or the bike-wrecking nerve-shattering cobblestone sections in northern France, there is fortunately another choice. *Brevetto Appenninico dei Nove Colli di km200 Trofeo Mauro Venturi* is the official long-winded title for a touring event which takes place in mid-

May in the sunny south of Italy, starting at Cesenatico on the Adriatic coast.

Anyone who decides to enter the event, enticed by the thoughts of sunshine and the Adriatic, should be warned in advance: a considerable measure of fitness and hill climbing ability is required. Only a minute proportion of the 200 kilometre course is covered on the level coastal strip. The vast majority of the route covers the hilly inland area of the Apennines, a mountain range which runs from the Po Valley throughout the length of the Italian peninsula. It is admittedly only a real mountain range in Tuscan Emilia, more or less on the same latitiude as Rome, where it forms a mighty rock wall known as the Gran Sasso Massif, with summits of around 3000 metres. Otherwise it may best be described as a hilly region, whose 1000 metre summits can hardly be awarded the status of mountains. The region is partly wooded and partly meadow land alternating with well-cultivated arable and pasture land. The highest point reached on this tour, 787 metres on the Colle Pugliano, is not very high, but if you remember that the start and finish line is at sea level, and that there are nine of these climbs, even though the rest are not quite so high, then you have some idea of what awaits you.

Riding through Cesenatico (0.0km), past the colourful sails of the fishing boats on the harbour canal, which was designed by no less a person that Leonardo da Vinci, the field, still intact, rolls inland towards Cesena (14km). Ahead of us lie small hills with tall cypresses, umberella pines, olive groves and remote farmsteads. Soon the road begins to climb, not on a regular gradient, but an almost wave-like undulation as we gain height. One or two kilometre climbs, with gradients of about 8%, but including short 12% stretches, are repeatedly interrupted by short descents, and soon the field, intact at the start, begins to spread out.

Beyond Polenta (26.5km) we reach the first summit, where the Tuscan Emilian Apennines run down towards the coast, and now the descent begins on a 14% gradient. Ahead the countryside opens out, becomes flatter, the hills are no longer so close together, and we are able to recover from our

Organisational Information

Date – Mid May

Distance – 200 and 130 kilometres

Total hillclimbs – About 3200 and 1500 metres

Highest climb – 12% on several longer sections

Gearing – 42x26/28

Start place – Cesenatico, a resort on the Adriatic coast between Ravenna and Rimini

Accommodation – Hotels and campsites in Cesenatico

Start time – Massed start at 6am

Entry fee – 40,000 lire

Feed stations – There are four feed stations *en route*

Participants – About 2000

Contact address – Gruppo Cicloturistico Fausto Coppi, Corso G Garibaldi 23, I-47042 Cesenati, Italy

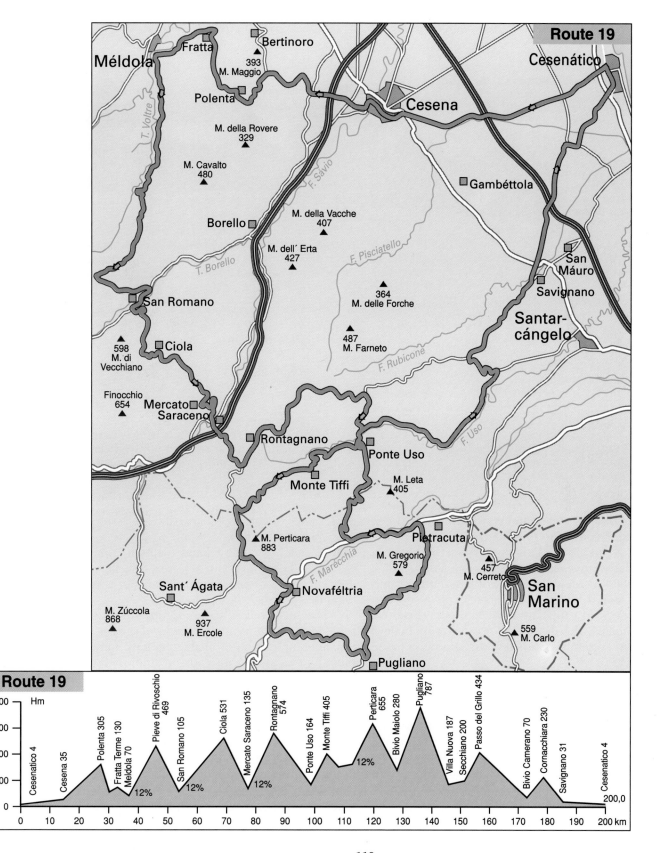

efforts on a level stretch, which runs between enormous fields of bright red poppies.

The easy rolling countryside becomes an almost five kilometre-long 6% climb, which soon increases to 12%, just before the second summit (45km). It almost seems as though the road drops away beneath our wheels, so steep is the descent. We can hardly believe the signposts showing the gradient to be 12%.

After San Romano (53km) we ride down into a broad valley, and in Mercato (76km) a climb of almost five kilometres with 12% gradients begins. Anyone who has imagined a pleasant coastal ride will by now realise he was mistaken. This route, on which the Italian professional championships were held, is really very demanding. In addition to the challenging route the heat makes the climbs more difficult, many riders might well

prefer one of the cooler northern classics. The short-route riders are able to breathe a sigh of relief, for in Sogliano (94.5km) they start their homeward journey, whilst we have only covered half of our course at Ponte Uso (98km).

The small yellow arrows signposting the route are leading us into the heart of the central Apennines, whose inhabitants have built their houses and farmsteads on hilltops far apart from each other. Once more we are climbing up 12% gradients. The rough asphalt is not always in good condition, and occasionally we have to absorb a heavy jolt through the handlebars. With these constant climbs and descents, we have long since stopped counting how many summits we have passed, but in Novafeltria (122km) the road surface gradually begins to improve, and our surroundings show more signs of life.

Poppies in full bloom add a splash of colour to the Apennines

A view of the Apennines in Tuscan Emilia

Jagged peaks rise like islands above the landscape, thickly wooded on three sides, but rocky and falling away steeply on the fourth side. With the ascent of the Col Pugliano (133.5km) we have completed the seventh and highest climb. In fact with its short 12% climbs and longer almost level sections it is fairly easy. Despite our fatigue, we cannot help admiring the castle of San Leo (136.5km), built precariously above the town at the top of a vertical rock-face, and we know the worst is behind us now.

The road descends towards Villa Nuova (145km). Rimini is signposted, and this conjours up images of sea and sandy beaches, but following the signs for Secchinano we must once again head inland. The road runs on the level to Secchinano (150km) and then leads to the five kilometre-climb of the Passo del Grillo (155km), including a 'harmless' 7% gradient. The countryside up here is remote, some of the mountain slopes are cultivated, the roads rough and bumpy, after the descent to Ponte Uso (159km) we realise we have ridden a wide loop. Just one small obstacle separates us from a well-earned dip in the Adriatic: the climb to Borgi (176.5km). There are two kilometres to climb on a 10% gradient before we reach the summit, and then the densely populated coastal strip spreads out below us, and the road heads down to Savignano (176.5km). There are orchards, houses, busy roads and crossings, and a flat road for the return to Cesnatico (200km). A swim in the Adriatic, however can only be recommended to hardy colleagues, for at this time of year the temperature has still not been raised by very much despite the warmer temperatures inland.

La Fausto Coppi–Cuneo
20
Italy

Riders on the descent from Bonette Pass. This photo was taken a few days before the event and on the day of the tour the road was not quite so bad, having been repaired

This tour through Italian Piemont, on the border with French Provence, was first staged as recently as 1987, and is dedicated to the Italian cycling hero Fausto Coppi. Anyone taking part should ideally be a mountain specialist in the mould of this double Tour de France winner, and five-times victor of the Tour of Italy, since a total hill climb figure of 4500 metres over a distance of 231 kilometres is involved and demands a great deal of endurance and persistence. Actually, there are events with a few more metres of hill climbing, but this tour can boast one really special feature: the 2802-metre Bonette Pass, the highest Alpine pass open to the public, which sits in defiance of its would-be conquerors.

The rider is just below the summit of the Lombard Pass, on the French-Italian border

We still have no idea what to expect when we arrive at the provincial capital of Cuneo after an hour's drive across the completely flat, maily sun-drenched plain of Piemont. Hardly one of the cyclists arriving here has noticed the range of dark mountain peaks, which seem to be so far away across the plain. They rise abruptly from the level ground, but it is not immediately obvious in the glare of the Italian sunshine. These mountains, however, are over 3000 metres high, and hardly 40 kilometres from Cuneo as the crow flies.

Those making preparations for the start on the huge Piazza Galimberti (0.0km) are mainly French and Italian riders familiar with the region. There is the usual air of ner-

Organisational Information

Date – Mid July

Distance – 231 kilometres

Total hill climbs – 4520 metres

Highest climb – 13% for about
3 kilometres on the Lombard Pass

Gearing – 42x26/28

Start place – Cuneo, Piazza Galimberti

Accommodation – Hotels and campsite in
Cuneo

Start time – Massed start at 6am

Entry fee – 50,000 lire

Feed stations – Three feed stations are *en
route*

Participants – About 1500

Contact address – Office de la Promo
Cuneo, Via XX Settembre 19, I-12100
Cuneo, Italy

Further information – The route was
changed in 1991. Previously it had
included the Angel Pass, the Vars Pass and
the Larche Pass. The distance was 243
kilometres, and the total hill climb was
3850 metres. It is not known if this route
change is permanent, so the current route
is described here, check with organisers
before you go

vous anticipation and hectic activity before
the massed start, but the Corso Nizza is wide
enough and offers plenty of space for the riders. No one is in a hurry for the ride is neu-
tralised at this stage and besides we are not
allowed to overtake the official vehicle leading the field out of town.

We leave the town on a straight level
road, and the hotels and suburban houses
give way to industrial estates. In Borgo San
Delmazzo (6.5km) we turn off the Stura
Valley, and the road remains almost flat, rising slightly now and then. After a good
hour's ride we reach Vinadio (36km), still
feeling very fresh. The real start to the tour is

here, where the road branches off for the
climb to the Lombard Pass. We have soon
crossed the valley and immediately things are
more difficult. The narrow road climbs at
anything up to 13% by way of tight hairpin
bends. This gradient is maintained for almost
1.5 kilometres, and then lessens. We cross a
mountain stream, and a further series of
hairpins with gradients of 10% and 12%
which only lessen at the Alpine Hostel of
Braccone (44km).

The climb remains difficult, we quickly
pass through the brief wider part of the valley, and another series of hairpin bends takes
us to the barren western slopes of the valley,
with the gradient increasing to 13%. A small
chapel (48km) indicates that half of the climb
has been completed, and an almost level section of about two kilometres provides some
time for us to recover. This is necessary, for
the road climbs once again at 12% through
more hairpin bends, before the gradient
finally eases off, and for the last few kilometres, it hardly reaches 6%.

The pass summit (59km) offers a barren,
scree-filled landscape, and this is the border
between Italy and France. The border post
does not appear until we have covered one
kilometre of the descent and the road is in
poor condition. Customs officers, enjoying
the spectacle offered by the speeding,
snaking line of colourful jerseys as we rush
down to the valley, wave us through for this
remote crossing is not busy at this time of
year, and is open only from June to October.
Just after the customs post, the road
improves in the new ski resort of Isola 2000.
The road has been improved, mainly for the
benefit of the skiing enthusiasts visiting the
area, there are two lanes now, but despite the
good surface, continuous descents and
numerous bends demand constant readiness
with the brakes.

In Isola (80km) we are glad to be back
on level ground, to shake the cramp from
our wrists, after constant braking, and to be
able to sit up after bending forward for so
long on the descent. The Tinée Valley, which
we are now climbing, is unimpressive and
sparsely populated. There are hardly any
noteworthy gradients: two hairpin bends
with a 6% gradient after the few houses of La
Haute Tinée (95km) is all there is to report

here. The main town in the valley represents the actual starting point for the ascent of the pass as we notice from the changing gradient as it rises to 7%.

After St Dalmas de Tende (100km) we enter the Mercantour National Park. The barren, rugged landscape is similar to that on the ascent of the Lombard Pass, but the valley is wider and the gradient not nearly so steep, being around 7%. The climb is also interspersed with level sections making it less difficult, but gradually the sheer distance takes its toll. There seems to be no prospect of an end. Before we reach Bousiéyas (108km) we have to negotiate a series of hairpins, where the gradient reaches 10%. We make use of the broad slopes; there is plenty of room for the road here, which climbs

between bare hillsides eroded by the weather. Turning the pedals almost monotonously we continue the climb, coming across white kilometre markings here and there, and an arrow with the inscription *Aqua* pointing to a spring. Wooden posts mark the line of the road, and then unexpectedly a small cutting appears as we reach the ridge (120km). We have arrived at the Restefond Pass, at an altitude of 2678 metres, and would be delighted to take the tempting opportunity to ride down the other side of the ridge, but we must complete the last section round the ridge's farthest peak. There is a 15% gradient for about 800 metres, which drains the last ounce of strength from our legs. Finally, we have reached the top, but we are too exhausted to appreciate the summit.

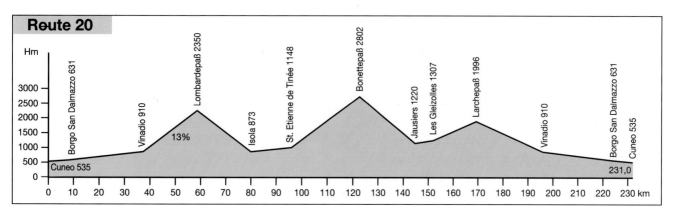

The descent down the northern side with its gradient of 12% is long, full of hairpin bends and because of the poor condition of the narrow road must be regarded as dangerous. The organisers have marked the worst of the road surface with white paint, but of course not all of the potholes could be marked, and so we are relieved to arrive safely in Jausiers (143.5km). We have completed the worst part of the tour and the ride through the Ubaye valley is similar to that of the Stura and the Tinée valleys. The landscape is barren, there is little traffic and the road climbs only slightly.

At the junction before we reach Les Gleizolles (151.5km) the last obstacle of the day lies ahead, the Larche Pass, or to use the Italian name, the Colle della Maddalena. There is no comparison with the severity of the previous climbs: an altitude change of 680 metres over 16.5 kilometres, a steady climb only exceeding 8% in Meyronnes (157.5km), the upper sections being easier. At the summit (168km), the finish line is still more than 60 kilometres away, but it is mainly downhill . The final part of the course is level, before our long day in the saddle comes to an end back in Cuneo (231km).

On the French side of the Lombard Pass. The descent is about to start

Riders must take great care, not only because of the poor road surfaces, as seen here on the upper part of the descent from the Croix-de-Fer Pass, but also because of the large number of participants

La Marmotte (the Marmot) is one of the best-known touring events in France. It is named after the little hibernating Alpine rodent, and you should be sure to have a good sleep first if you want to take part in this event, as you will have to climb 5000 metres on this 174 kilometre course. The names of the passes and mountain roads along the route have a special ring in cycling circles: the Croix-de-Fer Pass, involving 1300 metres of climb is the first hard test; the Galibier at 2646 metres is the third highest pass in the Alps and finally, the difficult ascent of the Alpe d'Huez, the usual finishing point for the Alpine stage of the Tour de France. The date for the tour is chosen specially because a few days later the professionals riding in the Tour de France will climb these passes on almost the same route; it certainly provides an added attraction to riders to make the long journey to try this tour.

Whilst the mountain slopes far above us are bathed in bright sunshine, it is still decidedly cool at 7.15am down in the Romanche Valley in the small town of Bourg d'Oisans. Most of the riders have been waiting for quite some time in the chill morning air, for anyone appearing just before the start will have to join the back of the long queue of waiting cyclists by the Genty supermarket. The start is on time and there is the usual jostling as 4000 cyclists set off together. Some lead cars are provided by the organisers, and there is a police escort, which will accompany the field for no further than the next crossroads in Rochetaillée (6km). There we begin the first long climb towards the Croix-de-Fer Pass. At first the road is fairly level (10km) but then it rises at 8% by the dam wall of the small reservoir at Allemond (11km). There is a short descent, and then it climbs up to 10% alternating with more level sections until we reach Rivier Allemond (20km)

Beyond the village there are steep descents with hairpin bends and gradients reaching 12%. On the slopes above us lighter coloured rocky areas are clearly visible, the result of a serious landslide, which has made it necessary to make a diversion. The descent lasts for a good kilometre, followed by a climb of similar length, before we rejoin the original road (25km) by way of two hairpin bends and a 12% gradient. The rest of the climb is completed at a more moderate gradient, mostly around 5% or less, before it climbs again to another small reservoir (30km), again at 8% with hairpin bends.

At the end of the reservoir we start a lengthy descent into the department de Savoie. The gradient maintains a steady 8% on the way to the first pass summit of the day (38.5km). The first feed station is up here, but it is firmly ignored by the leading riders. In this event, riders are chasing a time, which is recorded for every entrant by the organisers at the finish line. This appears not only on the results list, but is also published in the top French cycling magazine, *Le Cycle*. Those who are only concerned with completing the tour should allow themselves some time up here with this breathtaking Alpine

Organisational Information

Date – Early July

Distance – 174 kilometres

Total hill climbs – 5000 metres

Highest climb – 12% on a short stretch of the Croix-de-Fer Pass, and on short sections of the Galibier Pass

Gearing – 42x26/28

Start place – Bourg d'Oisans, by the Genty supermarket, about 45 kilometres east of Grenoble

Accommodation – Hotels and campsites in Bourg d'Oisans and surrounding area

Start time – Massed start at 7.15am

Entry fee – 160 French francs

Feed stations – There are two

Participants – About 4000

Contact address – Sports Organisation, Biviers BP4, F-38330 St Ismier, France

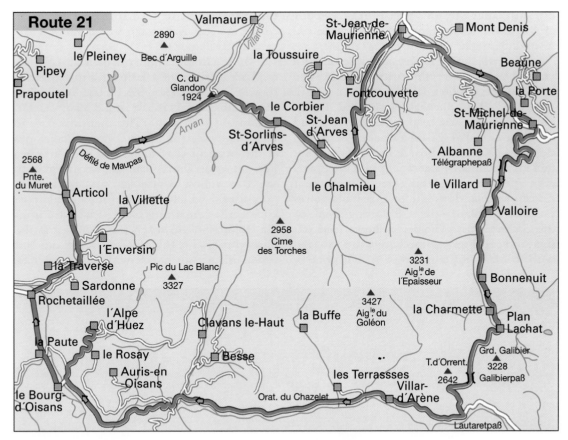

Route 21

panorama, before setting out on the descent.

Because of the sharp turns and hairpin bends, the poor condition of the road and the never-ending stream of riders this descent is not without danger. We are surrounded by shouts of 'A droite!' (keep right) 'A gauche!' (keep left) 'Attention!' (look out), along with an astonishing number of warning shouts in Dutch and Flemish. There are a couple of short tunnels on the lower sections which do little to improve the situation, and

even though the police down in St Jean-de-Maurienne have closed off the road to traffic, a few motorists always succeed in dodging the barriers so we must watch out for oncoming traffic as well.

The Arc Valley, which we entered at St Jean-de-Maurienne (68.5km) is wide, unremarkable and host to a very busy road. Its only advantage is that it is almost level. Two lanes alternate with a single lane in each direction, and when two lanes are available in

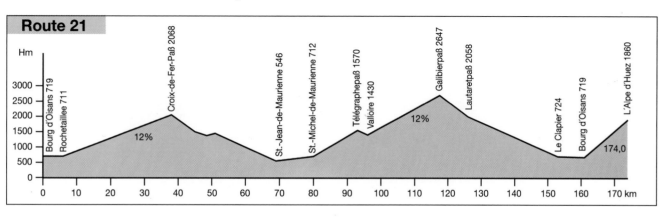

our direction one of them is reserved for cyclists now heading for the small industrial town of St Michel-de-Maurienne (80km).

We cross the River Arc, and ride under a viaduct as we leave the town (81km). The climb to the Galibier Pass begins, but before that, the Télégraphe Pass is reached during the long ascent. The road is well surfaced and climbs at a regular 8% up a wooded mountain slope with hairpin bends. At the halfway point (86km) a small feed station appears unexpectedly, and then, after the Télégraphe summit (93km) we ride downhill for three kilometres to Valloire (96km) – the real starting point for the Galibier Pass. There is a larger feed station here, and service mechanics are working hard to carry out minor repairs, but none of

the riders want to wait for too long here. There are still 1200 metres to climb over the next 18.5 kilometres.

After climbing out of town at 12% the road soon levels off a little, and the gradient remains mainly below 8% on the first half of the climb, as far as the small Plan Lachat Restaurant (105.5km). This then increases to 10% as we pass the barren, scree-filled slopes at the head of the valley, and even reaches 12% on some short sections. We are glad to see the yellow signposts set up by the organisers, which indicate the number of kilometres remaining before the pass summit. Before we do reach the entrance to the disused tunnel (115km), there is still one last series of hairpin bends with 10% and 12%

At the Galibier Pass soldiers distribute newspapers to protect riders from hypothermia on the long descent. A light windproof jacket would be a more modern alternative

gradients, and finally we reach the top (116.5km).

There is not enough space on the narrow ridge, where the riders are funnelled through narrow lines of barriers, and soldiers hand out newspapers to protect the body from hypothermia on the long descent. Some make use of these, but most prefer to put on their windcheaters, before making the descent to Lautaret Pass, with many bends and hairpins, and gradients reaching 15% on the upper sections. The road continues to descend for a long time after crossing the western side of the Lautaret Pass, no longer so steeply but the increase in traffic and some fairly long, poorly lit tunnels demand additional caution.

At Le Clapier (153.5km) we have reached the bottom of the valley, and a level seven kilometres lie ahead, before the start of the last climb. This can easily be described as consisting of 13.5 kilometres over 19 hairpin bends and a steady 10% gradient. Riding up it successfully is another matter, but if you have the opportunity to watch the professionals here a few days later, it will seem incredible how quickly they storm up these slopes. At the summit we can expect neither a cheque nor a cheeering crowd, but according to the time of day when we finish, there will be a smaller crowd of our fellow enthusiasts, who are equally proud to have completed the event.

Mobile service stations, like the one here at the start of the climb to the Galibier Pass, are able to carry out almost any repair

Alpine Tourist Trial
France

22

*H*ave you trained hard? Have you trained extremely hard? Have you already completed the Dolomite Marathon and the Ötztal Marathon, preferably in less than 10 hours? Then you can consider taking part in the Brevet de Randonneur des Alpes (BRA), a touring event which only takes place every second year. To be more exact, we are in fact discussing the Super Brevet de Randonneur des Alpes (Super BRA). This is the same event, extended by 50 kilometres and 75 metres of hill climb, from the normal 250 kilometres and 4650 metres of hill climbing.

It is not normal to start a tour at two o' clock in the morning, but this is the time when competitors in the super BRA leave the start area at the Palais des sports in Grenoble (0.0km). Starting with them are the few ladies, tandem riders and men over 50 years old, who have opted for the shorter BRA event. The rest of the group have little time to spare, they start according to age group at 3am or 4am, and finally a group of 'racers', who have chosen to complete the BRA in less than 12 hours, can leave at 6am. By the time the participants in the Super BRA have ridden through the Val d'Isère to Pontcharra (40km) in complete darkness, have turned off in La Rochette (50km) on to the mountain slopes of the Belledonne Range, and at Bourget-en-Huile (60km) have attacked the seven kilometre climb to the Grand Cucheron Pass (67km) with its four hairpins and a short section of 12% gradient, they will have climbed almost 1000 metres – of which they will lose 700 metres immediately on the descent to Epierre (85km).

Then comes the ride up the Arc Valley, in unremarkable surroundings as we can now make out in the early morning light, but the road is at least well-surfaced and almost level. In La Chambre (100km) we begin the climb out of the valley. Somehow we must accumulate some altitude, and the perfect opportunity is on the Glandon Pass. Rising majestically 1500 metres over 22 kilometres and with gradients of 15% these are dimensions that can really impress the cyclist. With a gradually increasing gradient we reach La Villard Martinan (110km), where dense forests hide any scenic views. A descent of 1.5 kilometres interrupts the climb, then gradient decreases to 8% and 10%, before it once

The descent from the Galibier Pass is in the shadow of the Meije, one of the most impressive mountains in the French Alps

After 207 kilometres supplies are replenished on the Galibier Pass

again becomes really difficult. On the last three kilometres before the summit, preceded by a series of hairpin bends, the gradient reaches 15%.

Happy the rider who has a 28 tooth rear sprocket! Triple chainwheels which some riders are using prove very useful on this course.

At the summit there is neither a restaurant nor a feed station, but we do have a fine

Organisational Information

Date – Mid July

Distance – 300 and 252 kilometres

Total hill climbs – 5400 or 4650 metres

Highest climb – 15% for about 1.5km on the Glandon Pass for the Super BRA. Since the Glandon Pass is not inlcuded in the BRA, the highest climbs on this route are around 12% on the Croix-de-Fer Pass and the Galibier Pass

Gearing – 42x28 or triple chainwheel

Start place – Palais de Sports, Grenoble. Signposted as BRA

Accommodation – Hotels and campsite in Grenoble

Start time – For Super BRA 2am, for BRA 2am to 6am according to age and ability

Entry fee – 70 French francs

Feed stations – There are three, which provide drinks

Participants – About 3500

Contact address – Arnaud Jules, 14 rue Eduard Amnet, F-38130 Echirolles, or, Cyclotouristes Grenobleois-BRA, BP 181-38004 Grenoble Cedex, France

Further information – The BRA and the super BRA take place only every second year. The 36th event was held on July 21, 1991

route through the Romanche Valley as they left Grenoble, and have climbed the western side of the Croix-de-Fer road. They have covered almost 75 kilometres, and have climbed a good 1800 metres.

The remaining section begins with a 2.5 kilometre section with gradients up to 7% and forms the approach to the Croix-de-Fer summit (125km). At the top there is another feed station, the first for BRA riders, the second, after the one on the Grand-Cucheron Pass, for the Super BRA riders. The choice offered is not too extravagant: tea coffee and other drinks, some fruit and muesli bars, so it's not a bad idea to take along some additional food in the pockets of your jersey. The road descends to St Jean-de-Maurienne (155km) over a distance of 30 kilometres with many twists and turns and on the upper sections in particular, the road is in poor condition. Back in the Arc Valley about 10 kilometres above La Chambre, the scenery is the same as before, perhaps the mountain-sides seem a little closer together, and the traffic has increased considerably, but the road is well-surfaced and almost level.

In St Michel-de-Maurienne (169km) we reach the junction for the Galibier Pass, whose 12.5km ascent starts with 888 metres to climb to the Télégraphe Pass (181.5km). There are 14 hairpin bends with a steady gradient between 8% and 10%. The road surface is good, passing through dense woodland, before we can finally rest our legs on the descent to Valloire (186.5km) and so recover a little from our exertions. It is worth pacing yourself at this stage as there are still 18.5 kilometres, over an altitude change of 1200 metres, and gradients of some 12% before we reach the summit ahead. These are statistics which describe the route, but say nothing about the strength and will power which are necessary to fight up to the summit, which sits between shimmering black and ochre scree-slopes.

Leaving Valloire we climb at 12%, but then the gradients ease, and longer, more level sections follow as we approach the Restaurant Plan Lachat (196km). Again there is a series of hairpin bends with 12% gradients, a long section at 10%, and as we pass the entrance to the disused Scheitel Tunnel (201km), the last tortuous two kilometres

view of the peak of Mont Blanc far away in the north-east. We begin a short descent, which ends when we join the road to the Croix-de-Fer Pass after 500 metres. Here we meet the BRA riders who took the direct

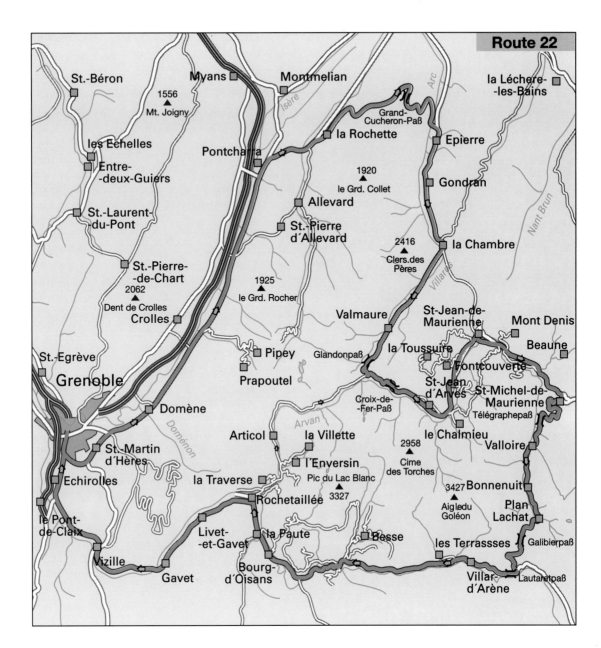

St.-Béron

Myans

Montmelian

la Léchere-
-les-Bains

Isère

1556
▲
Mt. Joigny

Arc

Grand-
Cucheron-Paß

les Echelles

Pontcharra

la Rochette

Epierre

Entre-
-deux-Guiers

1920
▲
le Grd. Collet

Gondran

Nant Brun

St.-Laurent-
du-Pont

Allevard

St.-Pierre
d´Allevard

2416
▲
Clers.des
Pères

la Chambre

St.-Pierre
-de-Chart

1925
▲
le Grd. Rocher

Villardⁿ

2062
▲
Dent de Crolles

Crolles

Valmaure

St-Jean-de-
Maurienne

Mont Denis

St.-Egrève

Pipey

Glandonpaß

la Toussuire

Beaune

Fontcouverte

Grenoble

Prapoutel

St-Jean
d´Arves

St-Michel-de-
Maurienne

Domène

Croix-de-
-Fer-Paß

Télégraphepaß

Doménon

Arvan

Articol

la Villette

2958
▲
Cime
des Torches

le Chalmieu

Valloire

St.-Martin
d´Hères

l´Enversin

Pic du Lac Blanc

3427
▲
Aigle du
Goléon

Bonnenuit

Echirolles

la Traverse

Rochetaillée

3327

Plan
Lachat

le Pont-
de-Claix

la Paute

Besse

les Terrassses

Galibierpaß

Livet-
-et-Gavet

Vizille

Gavet

Bourg-
d´Oisans

Villar-
d´Arène

Lautaretpaß

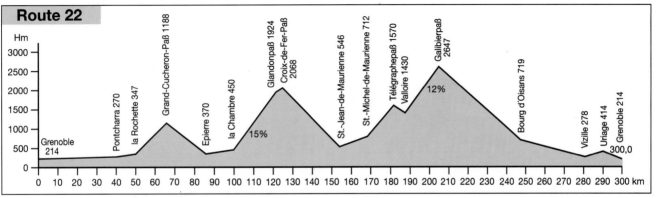

stretch ahead of us, with hairpin bends and gradients between 10% and 12%. Sometimes dramas are acted out up here, as some riders, tortured by cramp, with aching backs and legs, call upon the last remnants of their strength. But there is no one to help them, since the others are suffering in the same way. There is no one to whom you can complain, for as it says in the leaflet published by the organisers: 'You do it for your own pleasure'.

At the pass (203km), the world may look different, where the view of the mighty hanging glacier of the Barre des Ecrins is one of the most impressive panoramas to be seen in the whole of the Alps. There is also a feed station, but nevertheless we shall soon be leaving this cool and windy spot, at 2647 metres the third highest Alpine pass after the Restfond/Bonette Pass and the Iseran Pass. The finishing line is still 100 kilometres away, but the next 46 are all downhill across the southern side of the Galibier Pass, and then over the western slopes of the Lautaret Pass to Bourg d'Oisans (249km). Then the road to Vizille (281km) remains level or descends slightly. Those who have come this far will also be able to manage the last 150 metres of hill climb to Uriage (290km). There is no alternative, in fact, for the support vehicle is only intended for emergencies. In Grenoble we have completed what the organisers call 'a somewhat hard but unforgettable bike trip'. By this they mean the Brevet de Randonneur des Alpes – for the Super Brevet de Randonneur des Alpes words fail them.

Just below the summit of the Croix-de-Fer Pass, this group of riders are attempting to complete the BRA in less than 12 hours

Den store Styrkeprøven   23
(The great test of strength)
Trondheim–Oslo ▬
Norway

Riders bunch together to maintain a steady tempo, as here on the Dovrefjell

*E*ven by car, 540 kilometres is a long way. The bus or the train would be an alternative means of transport, and anyone in a hurry would consider flying. A bicycle is by no means suitable for such a distance, especially when a time limit of 40 hours is imposed. Every year however, more than 5000 riders take up the challenge of completing this tour from Trondheim to Oslo, simply to receive a certificate bearing their name and their total time for the ride, along with a tour medal. There may be no logical reason for this, but one is not needed, for only when you have experienced this tour for yourself, which is rightly called the Great Test of Strength, can you appreciate the achievement.

After 380 kilometres it is permissible to push your bike or accept the help of your companion

It is raining in Trondheim and the temperature is eight degrees; it will not exceed 13 degrees during the day, and the rain will stop for only a short time. Not exactly ideal weather for cycling, and yet very few of the 5000 plus participants withdraw from the start. They throng in the area outside the brick built Nidaros Cathedral, one of the most notable European church buildings, in which every Norwegian king has been crowned. The riders are checked for lights and crash helmets, and wait to be sent on their long journey in groups of 75 at two minute intervals.

The first kilometres take us through Trondheim, where the E6 is wide, having four lanes at this point. A climb of about two kilometres at 5% leads out of town, a long descent follows, and we turn off for Oslo at a roundabout (14.5km). We read 'Oslo 527km' on a road sign, a figure best forgotten at this stage.

There are green meadows, woodland and typical wooden houses painted deep red – there is nothing really remarkable about our surroundings. At first the road seems to rise and fall like waves, climbing 100 to 200 metres at around 7% only to fall away immediately, but beyond Kval (25km), it levels out again. The route remains flat until we reach Soknedal (63km), there are a couple of 4% gradients, which make for an easy ride. The valley is not very wide but densely wooded, with occasional rocky crags, where a river by the name of Gaula carries its dark brown waters to the Norwegian sea.

In Garli (72km) we come across the first feed station: tables groan under the weight of sandwiches, fruit and drink will fulfil the energy requirements of all the riders from first to last. The leading riders have been travelling for less than two hours. They want to beat the existing record of 13 hours and 54 minutes, and do not stop, in contrast to the last riders, who do not arrive until noon. As we head towards Driva (127km) and the

Organisational Information

Date – Late June

Distance – 540 kilometres

Total hill climbs – About 1500 metres

Highest climb – 7% on short stretches

Start place – Nidaros Cathedral, Trondheim

Accommodation – Hotels and campsite in Trondheim

Start time – Between 8am and 10.36am in groups of 75 at two minute intervals.

Entry fee – 600 kroners. Riders who do not hold a licence issued by the Norwegian Cycling Fedaration must purchase a temporary licence costing 50kr. Support vehicles must be registered

Feed stations – There are 10 feed stations *en route*

Participants – About 5000

Contact address – Oslo Cyklekrets, Idrettens Hus, Ekeberg veien 101, N-1178 Oslo, Norway

Further information – The event must be completed within 40 hours. In 1991 the fastest times were: 13 hrs 57 mins (men), 18 hours 14 mins (women). Of 5242 starters, 4027 finished. The event is very well organised: there are feed stations offering food, first aid and spares. At four stations matresses, showers and hot meals are available. Service vans, marked Dommer/Service, patrol the route to provide break down assistance. Head protection and lights are compulsory

next *Matsstasjon* as the feed stations are called here, there are some easy climbs, the road is mainly level, and there are a few descents. Almost without noticing, we have climbed 400 metres over the distance covered so far. Leaving the feed station, we glance at the signpost where the number of kilometres to the next one is shown – it says '52km'.

There is no reason to feel worried, the road continues more or less level, and allows us to make good progress as usual, before the valley narrows at about 150 kilometres. The climb to the Doverfjell begins. It is not steep at any point, hardly ever above 5%, and less than that for long stretches, but at 10 kilometres it is a long haul. A further problem occurs at this point: the traffic. Shortly after leaving Trondheim the E6 narrows to two lanes, it is not very wide and carries a lot of traffic. Larger groups and the lead riders are lucky, they are protected by the organisers' cars, or by support vehicles. If the field splits up, however, and is strung out in single file, vehicles begin to force their way in between the cyclists. It is worst for those riders who started last the so called green groups, travelling without support vehicles, and no protection from thundering traffic. For them the narrow hard shoulder at the edge of the carriageway

We are now riding on what is perhaps the most attractive section of the route, where the undulating road leads on to Hjerkinn (164.5km), the highest point on the route at 1022 metres. Up here there is a plateau, with small bushes, rocks covered in moss and lichen, and small trees – the taller trees have been bowed by the wind. In the distance there are snow-covered mountain ridges, which hardly seem any higher than our present position. The road stays at this altitude for a considerable distance as we pass through the third feed station (175.5km), eventually descending at 5% after 198 kilometres, and approaching Dombas (201km).

We turn into the Gudbrand Valley, which we follow now for more than 150 kilometres to Lillehammer (354km). This is Norway's most famous valley, which reflects the typical rural landscape of the country. The road is narrow and densely wooded on some stretches, and then widens out again, with plenty of space for green pasture land, fertile fields and splendid villages. The River Lagen flows through the valley, forming a series of lakes along its length. Its fame goes back to the middle ages, when the kings passed through this region on their way to Trondheim for their coronation. On the

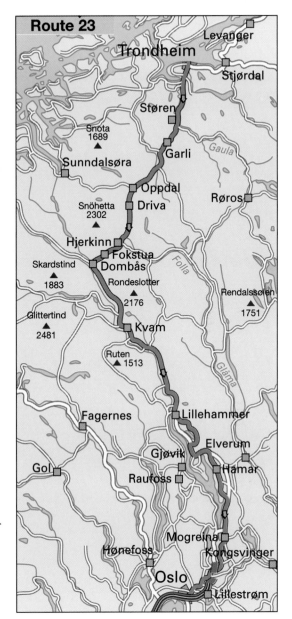

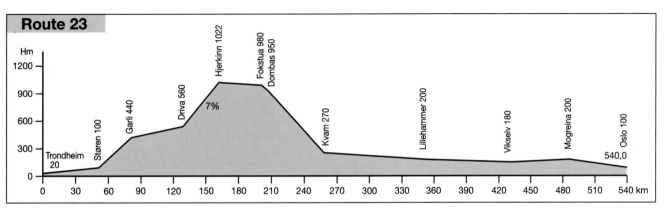

return journey they were faced with not a single gradient, but with a flat or gently falling road on the more than 150 kilometre section between Dombas and Lillehammer, just as we are today.

The fastest riders will have arrived at the finish in Oslo by now, but the majority of us are still on this Dombas–Lillehammer section of the route, and many spend time between dawn and dusk on this road. It does not become really dark, but visibility is poor; it is sufficient for us to be aware of our immediate

In the Gudbrand Valley after Lillehammer. Two riders in the green group, riding without support

in addition to hot meals, showers, massage and beds are available. This is the time which makes the greatest demands upon the endurance of the rider, and which is survived by each competitor in his own way. Just before Faberg (345.5km) the E6 is left for the first time, but only temporarily, since we rejoin it twice. The scenery around is rural, with meadows, pasture land, cultivated fields and tiny hamlets, a scene which does not change before Oslo. The characteristics of the route will not change very much, from Lillehammer onwards there are more climbs. They do not have difficult gradients, mainly around 3% or 4%, one increases to 6% for a short time. By far the greater part of the route is level, or downhill.

These gradients do, however, disturb your rhythm, and many riders who at first reached for the gear lever in order not to waste any effort will sooner or later change up again and ride the rest of the route at a steady tempo. Others set themselves the next feed station as a goal, they are located every 40 kilometres, and after every stop it gets more difficult to climb back in the saddle. It takes a while to find a riding position that's comfortable. Other riders use the signposts as a guide and calculate the time needed to finish, although time has lost its meaning for us. But we all have one common cause, and that is to complete the course, and the going is agonisingly slow. A few give up, but most persist. If there is a breakdown we can count on being found by one of the service cars, which drive up and down the route.

We know we are close to Oslo as the traffic increases, then the boundary sign comes into view (526km), but there are still 14 kilometres from here to the finish. Only on the last kilometre is one lane of the dual carriageway reserved for competitors, it takes us right up to the barriers and spectators who applaud every rider. A corner is taken from our start number as information for the computer-assisted time cards, and we soon receive our certificate and medal in a nearby building. These will surely be given place of honour in every home, for they will act as a reminder of the greatest endurance test possible for any cyclist.

vehicles, will be hard pressed to keep within the time limit of 40 hours

surroundings but cyclists are difficult to spot by other road users at this time of night. For riders without support vehicles, it is advisable to spend the time between midnight and 3am at one of the feed stations, in Kvam, for instance (263km) or Ringebu (298km) where